GIGA BOOSTER
FOR THE TOEIC® L&R TEST

Koji Hayakawa   Naoyuki Bamba

KINSEIDO

Kinseido Publishing Co., Ltd.

3-21 Kanda Jimbo-cho, Chiyoda-ku,
Tokyo 101-0051, Japan

First published 2023 by Kinseido Publishing Co., Ltd.

Text design: Asahi Media International Inc.

🎧 音声ファイル無料ダウンロード

https://www.kinsei-do.co.jp/download/4183

この教科書で 🎧 DL 00 の表示がある箇所の音声は、上記 URL または QR コードにて
無料でダウンロードできます。自習用音声としてご活用ください。

▶ PC からのダウンロードをお勧めします。スマートフォンなどでダウンロードされる場合は、
　ダウンロード前に「解凍アプリ」をインストールしてください。

▶ URL は **検索ボックスではなくアドレスバー (URL 表示欄)** に入力してください。

▶ お使いのネットワーク環境によっては ダウンロードできない場合があります。

◎ CD 00　左記の表示がある箇所の音声は、教室用 CD（Class Audio CD）に収録されています。

はじめに

本書は、*TOEIC*® Listening and Reading Test（以下、TOEIC L&Rテスト）のスコア400前後レベルの学習者を対象として作成されています。また、著者の豊富なTOEIC指導経験および受験経験や教材作成経験から、学習のしやすさを追求したのみでなく、TOEIC L&Rテストに必須の単語や文法のほか、各パートの基本的な出題パターンを網羅することを意識して作成されています。

本書の特徴は3つあります。1つめは「トピック別に学べる」ことです。UnitはすべてTravelやMediaなどトピック別となっているため、同じトピックで使われる単語やフレーズを効率的に学べます。さらに、学習した単語やフレーズがUnit内のすべてのパートの学習を通して何度も繰り返し登場しますので、定着しやすい仕掛けがあります。

2つめの特徴は「たくさんの問題を解く練習ができる」ことです。各Unitでは、前半のPractice!でディクテーションや書き込みなどにより各パートのポイントを学んだ後に、後半で本番形式のMini Testに取り組みます。すでに学習した内容を踏まえて多くの問題に取り組むことで、解答パターンをつかむことができ、身につけた知識をスキルへと高めやすくなります。

3つめの特徴が「解きっぱなしにせず、復習が行える」ことです。教授用資料に掲載されているReview Sheetを活用することで、一度解いたMini Testに別の角度から取り組み、より深く内容の定着を図ることができます。解けた問題についてはさらに英文の理解を深めることができますし、解けなかった問題についても、内容の理解を高めることによって似たタイプの問題に正解しやすくなります。

TOEIC L&Rテストに登場する内容は、どれも日常的に使われているものです。映画を見ているときに出合うこともありますし、海外旅行中に出合うこともあります。そして、卒業後の近い将来、TOEICを通して学んだ英語を仕事で使いこなしているかもしれません。

本書が学生のみなさんの英語力向上およびTOEIC L&Rテストのスコアアップのお役に立てることを願っています。

著者を代表して
早川幸治

本書は CheckLink（チェックリンク）対応テキストです。

CheckLinkのアイコンが表示されている設問は、CheckLink に対応しています。
CheckLink を使用しなくても従来通りの授業ができますが、特色をご理解いただき、授業活性化のためにぜひご活用ください。

CheckLink の特色について

　大掛かりで複雑な従来のe-learningシステムとは異なり、CheckLink のシステムは大きな特色として次の３点が挙げられます。

1. これまで行われてきた教科書を使った授業展開に大幅な変化を加えることなく、専門的な知識なしにデジタル学習環境を導入することができる。
2. PC教室やCALL教室といった最新の機器が導入された教室に限定されることなく、普通教室を使用した授業でもデジタル学習環境を導入することができる。
3. 授業中での使用に特化し、教師・学習者双方のモチベーション・集中力をアップさせ、授業自体を活性化することができる。

▶教科書を使用した授業に「デジタル学習環境」を導入できる

　本システムでは、学習者は教科書のCheckLink のアイコンが表示されている設問にPCやスマートフォン、アプリからインターネットを通して解答します。そして教師は、授業中にリアルタイムで解答結果を把握し、正解率などに応じて有効な解説を行うことができるようになっています。教科書自体は従来と何ら変わりはありません。解答の手段としてCheckLink を使用しない場合でも、従来通りの教科書として使用して授業を行うことも、もちろん可能です。

▶教室環境を選ばない

　従来の多機能なe-learning教材のように学習者側の画面に多くの機能を持たせることはせず、「解答する」ことに機能を特化しました。PCだけでなく、一部タブレット端末やスマートフォン、アプリからの解答も可能です。したがって、PC教室やCALL教室といった大掛かりな教室は必要としません。普通教室でもCheckLink を用いた授業が可能です。教師はPCだけでなく、一部タブレット端末やスマートフォンからも解答結果の確認をすることができます。

▶授業を活性化するための支援システム

　本システムは予習や復習のツールとしてではなく、授業中に活用されることで真価を発揮する仕組みになっています。CheckLink というデジタル学習環境を通じ、教師と学習者双方が授業中に解答状況などの様々な情報を共有することで、学習者はやる気を持って解答し、教師は解答状況に応じて効果的な解説を行う、という好循環を生み出します。CheckLink は、普段の授業をより活力のあるものへと変えていきます。

　上記３つの大きな特色以外にも、掲示板などの授業中に活用できる機能を用意しています。従来通りの教科書としても使用はできますが、ぜひCheckLink の機能をご理解いただき、普段の授業をより活性化されたものにしていくためにご活用ください。

CheckLink の使い方

CheckLink は、PC や一部のタブレット端末、スマートフォン、アプリを用いて、この教科書にある ↻CheckLink のアイコン表示のある設問に解答するシステムです。
・初めて CheckLink を使う場合、以下の要領で**「学習者登録」**と**「教科書登録」**を行います。
・一度登録を済ませれば、あとは毎回「**ログイン画面**」から入るだけです。CheckLink を使う教科書が増えたときだけ、改めて**「教科書登録」**を行ってください。

CheckLink URL

https://checklink.kinsei-do.co.jp/student/

登録は CheckLink 学習者用 **アプリ**が便利です。ダウンロードはこちらから ▶▶▶

▶学習者登録 (PC /タブレット/スマートフォンの場合)

①上記 URL にアクセスすると、右のページが表示されます。学校名を入力し「ログイン画面へ」を選択してください。
PCの場合は「PC用はこちら」を選択して PC 用ページを表示します。同様に学校名を入力し「ログイン画面へ」を選択してください。

②ログイン画面が表示されたら「**初めての方はこちら**」を選択し「学習者登録画面」に入ります。

③自分の学籍番号、氏名、メールアドレス (学校のメールなど **PC メールを推奨**) を入力し、次に**任意のパスワード**を8桁以上20桁未満 (半角英数字) で入力します。なお、学籍番号はパスワードとして使用することはできません。

④「パスワード確認」は、❸で入力したパスワードと同じものを入力します。

⑤最後に「登録」ボタンを選択して登録は完了です。次回からは、「ログイン画面」から学籍番号とパスワードを入力してログインしてください。

▶教科書登録

①ログイン後、メニュー画面から「教科書登録」を選び（PCの場合はその後「新規登録」ボタンを選択）、「教科書登録」画面を開きます。

②教科書と受講する授業を登録します。
教科書の最終ページにある、**教科書固有番号**のシールをはがし、印字された**16桁の数字とアルファベット**を入力します。

③授業を担当される先生から連絡された**11桁の授業ID**を入力します。

④最後に「登録」ボタンを選択して登録は完了です。

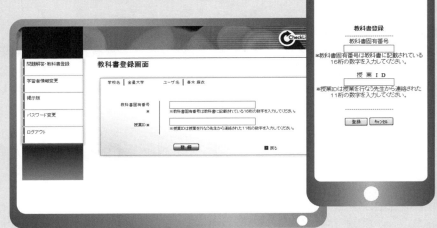

⑤実際に使用する際は「教科書一覧」（PCの場合は「教科書選択画面」）の該当する教科書名を選択すると、「問題解答」の画面が表示されます。

▶問題解答

①問題は教科書を見ながら解答します。この教科書の CheckLink のアイコン表示のある設問に解答できます。

②問題が表示されたら選択肢を選びます。

③表示されている問題に解答した後、「解答」ボタンを選択すると解答が登録されます。

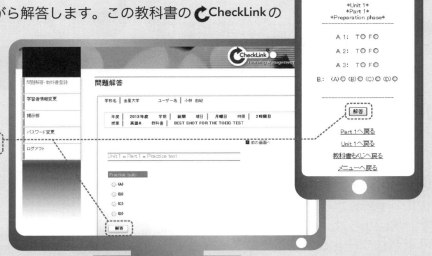

▶CheckLink 推奨環境

PC

推奨 OS
　Windows 7, 10 以降
　MacOS X 以降

推奨ブラウザ
　Internet Explorer 8.0 以上
　Firefox 40.0 以上
　Google Chrome 50 以上
　Safari

携帯電話・スマートフォン
　3G 以降の携帯電話（docomo, au, softbank）
　iPhone, iPad（iOS9 〜）
　Android OS スマートフォン、タブレット

・最新の推奨環境についてはウェブサイトをご確認ください。
・上記の推奨環境を満たしている場合でも、機種によってはご利用いただけない場合もあります。また、
　推奨環境は技術動向等により変更される場合があります。

▶CheckLink 開発

CheckLink は奥田裕司 福岡大学教授、正興 IT ソリューション株式会社、株式会社金星堂に
よって共同開発されました。

CheckLink は株式会社金星堂の登録商標です。

CheckLink の使い方に関するお問い合わせは…

正興 IT ソリューション株式会社　CheckLink 係

e-mail checklink@seiko-denki.co.jp

Contents

Unit 1 Travel

TOEIC Vocabularies & Phrases:「旅行」に関する語句・表現を覚える

PART 1: 人物の動作① 1人のパターン

PART 2: WH疑問文① Who で始まる疑問文

PART 3: 会話の話題を聞き取る

PART 4: トークの話題を聞き取る

PART 5: 品詞① 名詞

PART 6: 語彙問題① やさしめの語彙

PART 7: 概要に関する問題① 目的や概要は冒頭で述べられる

Unit 2 Dining Out

TOEIC Vocabularies & Phrases:「食事」に関する語句・表現を覚える

PART 1: 人物の動作② 2人のパターン

PART 2: WH疑問文② Where で始まる疑問文

PART 3: 会話が行われている場所を特定する

PART 4: トークが行われている場所を特定する

PART 5: 品詞② 形容詞

PART 6: 語彙問題② 難しめの語彙

PART 7: 詳細情報に関する問題① 設問のキーワードを参考にする

Unit 3 Daily Life

TOEIC Vocabularies & Phrases:「日常生活」に関する語句・表現を覚える

PART 1: 人物の動作③ 3人以上のパターン

PART 2: WH疑問文③ When で始まる疑問文

PART 3: 会話から話し手の働いている場所や部門を推測する

PART 4: トークから話し手の働いている場所や部門を推測する

PART 5: 品詞③ 副詞

PART 6: 語彙問題③ まとめ

PART 7: 推測させる問題① キーワードを参考に情報を読み取る

TOEIC® Listening and Reading テストについて

- ●TOEICとは、Test of English for International Communicationの略称で、「英語によるコミュニケーション能力」を総合的に評価するテストです。
- ●実際のテストでは、リスニング100問（約45分間）、リーディング100問（75分間）の計200問を約2時間で解きます（休憩はありません）。
- ●マークシート方式で、問題はすべて英語で構成されています。
- ●出題内容は、日常的な話題からビジネスのシチュエーションまで多岐にわたりますが、特殊なビジネスの知識を必要とする問題は出題されません。
- ●スコアは10～990まで5ポイント刻みで算出されます。

問題形式について

リスニングセクション（約45分間：100問）＊	
PART 1	**写真描写問題：6問** ・1枚の写真について4つの短い英文を聞いて、最も適切に描写しているものを選びます。 ・英文は印刷されていません。
PART 2	**応答問題：25問** ・1つの質問（または発言）と3つの応答を聞いて、最も適切な応答を選びます。 ・質問および応答は印刷されていません。
PART 3	**会話問題：39問（1つの会話につき3つの設問×13セット）** ・2人または3人の人物による会話と設問を聞いて、選択肢から最も適切な答えを選びます。 ・会話中の表現の意図を問う問題が出題されます（意図問題）。 ・注文書、グラフ、地図など図表を見て答える問題が出題されます（図表問題）。 ・会話は印刷されていません（設問および選択肢は印刷されています）。
PART 4	**説明文問題：30問（1つの説明文につき3つの設問×10セット）** ・アナウンスやナレーションなどのトークと設問を聞いて、選択肢から最も適切な答えを選びます。 ・トーク中の表現の意図を問う問題が出題されます（意図問題）。 ・注文書、グラフ、地図など図表を見て答える問題が出題されます（図表問題）。 ・トークは印刷されていません（設問および選択肢は印刷されています）。

＊音声はアメリカ、イギリス、カナダ、オーストラリアの発音です。

	リーディングセクション（75分間：100問）	
PART 5	**短文穴埋め問題：30問** ・短い文の中に空所が1つあります。 ・空所に入る最も適切な選択肢を選んで文を完成させます。	
PART 6	**長文穴埋め問題：16問** ・長文の中に空所が4つあります。 ・空所に入る最も適切な選択肢を選んで文を完成させます。 ・文書中に入る適切な語句または文を選択する問題が出題されます（文選択問題）。	
PART 7	**読解問題：54問（1つの文書：29問、複数の文書：25問）** ・Eメールや広告、記事などのさまざまな文書と設問を読み、選択肢から最も適切な答えを選びます。 ・1つの文書（シングルパッセージ）を読んで答えるものと、2～3つの関連する文書（ダブルパッセージ／トリプルパッセージ）を読んで答えるものの2タイプがあります。 ・チャット形式など、複数の人物によるやりとりに関する問題が出題されます。 ・文書中の表現の意図を問う問題が出題されます（意図問題）。 ・文を挿入する適切な位置を選択する問題が出題されます（文挿入問題）。 ・1つの文書では2~4問、複数の文書では5問の設問があります。	

†一般受験の*TOEIC*® Listening and Reading 公開テストのほかに、企業や学校向けの団体特別受験「IPテスト」があります。IPテストでは過去に公開テストで出題された問題を使用します。

TOEIC学習 "3 Days × 7 Sets" スケジュール

魔法の数字「3」でスタートする習慣化への道

早川幸治

習慣化に必要なことはスケジュール作りです。「いつ」「どこで」「何をするか」を明確にすることで、モチベーションや意志に頼ることなく、スケジュール通りに学習しやすくなります。まずは3日分のスケジュールを立てて、実践してみてください。最初に立てた計画通りにいかなかった場合は、軌道修正をかけてください。そして、次の3日分、さらに3日分とこれを7回繰り返すと3日×7で21日（3週間）です。3週間続けば習慣になります。そして、この3週間×4の12週間（3カ月）で、結果が見えてきます。スポーツもダイエットも英語学習も、就職後の企業活動も、3カ月が1つのカタマリになっていることが多くあります。そして、この3カ月×4が12カ月（1年）です。1年続けるためには3カ月続ける必要があります。3カ月続けるためには3週間続ける必要があります。3週間続けるためには、今日から3日続ける必要があります。まずは3日からスタートしましょう！

> スケジュールのコツは流れの中に入れてしまうことです。
> 「いつ」に関しては、7:30 という時間でもよいですし、「歯磨きをした後」という「何かの前後」でも効果的です。「通学の電車に乗ったら」であれば、「いつ／どこで」が同時に明確になります。

まずは3日分のスケジュールを立てて、7回繰り返してみよう！

1	**Day 1**	いつ／どこで： 何をする：
	Day 2	いつ／どこで： 何をする：
	Day 3	いつ／どこで： 何をする：
2	**Day 4**	いつ／どこで： 何をする：
	Day 5	いつ／どこで： 何をする：
	Day 6	いつ／どこで： 何をする：

	Day 7	いつ／どこで： 何をする：
3	Day 8	いつ／どこで： 何をする：
	Day 9	いつ／どこで： 何をする：
	Day 10	いつ／どこで： 何をする：
4	Day 11	いつ／どこで： 何をする：
	Day 12	いつ／どこで： 何をする：
	Day 13	いつ／どこで： 何をする：
5	Day 14	いつ／どこで： 何をする：
	Day 15	いつ／どこで： 何をする：
	Day 16	いつ／どこで： 何をする：
6	Day 17	いつ／どこで： 何をする：
	Day 18	いつ／どこで： 何をする：
	Day 19	いつ／どこで： 何をする：
7	Day 20	いつ／どこで： 何をする：
	Day 21	いつ／どこで： 何をする：

TOEIC
Vocabularies & Phrases

Unit 1 Travel

次のUnit 1に登場するTOEIC頻出語句＆フレーズです。

> **Step 1** 意味を確認した上で、音声に続いて音読してみましょう。
> **Step 2** 再度音声を聞きながら、意味を思い出してみましょう。

🎧 DL002 💿 CD1-02

☐☐☐ aisle seat	☐☐☐	通路側の席
☐☐☐ available	☐☐☐	形 空いている、入手できる
☐☐☐ board	☐☐☐	動 乗り込む
☐☐☐ book	☐☐☐	動 予約する
☐☐☐ complete	☐☐☐	動 完了する、記入する
		形 完全な、完成した
☐☐☐ confirm	☐☐☐	動 確認する
☐☐☐ delay	☐☐☐	名 遅延　動 遅らせる
☐☐☐ depart	☐☐☐	動 出発する
☐☐☐ destination	☐☐☐	名 目的地
☐☐☐ due to	☐☐☐	……が原因で
☐☐☐ form	☐☐☐	名 用紙
☐☐☐ frequent	☐☐☐	形 頻繁な
☐☐☐ itinerary	☐☐☐	名 旅行日程（表）
☐☐☐ luggage	☐☐☐	名 手荷物
☐☐☐ passenger	☐☐☐	名 乗客
☐☐☐ present	☐☐☐	動 提示する
☐☐☐ reservation	☐☐☐	名 予約
☐☐☐ sightseeing	☐☐☐	名 観光
☐☐☐ travel agency	☐☐☐	旅行代理店
☐☐☐ vehicle	☐☐☐	名 乗り物

Travel

学習目標
- ☐ 「旅行」に関する語句・表現を覚える
- ☐ 名詞を学ぶ

PART 1 写真描写問題

人物の動作① 1人のパターン

人物の動作を表す文では現在進行形が多く使われます。

The man **is standing** near the counter.（男性がカウンターの近くに立っている）

動詞や目的語のほか、場所を示す単語の聞き取りがポイントとなります。

Practice!  CheckLink DL003 CD1-03

音声を聞いて空所の語句を書き取り、写真を最も適切に表す選択肢を選びましょう。

(A) The man is _____ an _____.

(B) The man is _____ his _____.

(C) The man is _____ at the _____.

(D) The man is _____ near the _____.

PART 2 応答問題

WH疑問文① Whoで始まる疑問文

Whoは人物を問う疑問詞のため、応答は人物の名前や役職になることが多くあります。また、Whoseも基本的に人物が問われているため、WhoやWhoseの聞き取りに加え、その後に続く内容を聞き取ることで質問の意味がわかります。

Practice! CheckLink DL004 ~ 005 CD1-04 ~ CD1-05

音声を聞いて空所の語句を書き取り、最も適切な応答の選択肢を選びましょう。

1. Who _____ _____ a _____ _____ to Canada?

    (A) The _____.

    (B) For _____ _____.

    (C) Not _____.

2. Who did you _____ about the _____?

    (A) _____ _____.

    (B) The _____ _____.

    (C) I _____ _____ for that.

PART 3 会話問題

Practice!

音声を聞いて空所の語句を書き取り、設問に対する最も適切な選択肢を選びましょう。

1. ⟲CheckLink 🎧 DL006 ⊙ CD1-06

W: Hello, I'd like to _____ a _____ for next Saturday.

M: We have two _____ _____ _____.

What are the speakers discussing?

(A) A sightseeing spot

(B) A hotel reservation

(C) A travel itinerary

(D) Public transportation

2. ⟲CheckLink 🎧 DL007 ⊙ CD1-07

M: Hello, I'd like to _____ a _____ for the 3 o'clock _____ to Tokyo.

W: Sure. Would you like to have a _____ seat or an _____ seat?

What is the topic of the conversation?

(A) A hotel

(B) A flight delay

(C) A ticket

(D) Departure time

PART 4 説明文問題

> **トークの話題を聞き取る**
> Part 3と同様、冒頭を理解することでトークの「目的」「聞き手」「場所」「概要」などがわかることが多いので、冒頭部分は集中して聞きましょう。特に概要がわかることで、その後の内容理解に大きく役立ちます。

Practice!

音声を聞いて空所の語句を書き取り、設問に対する最も適切な選択肢を選びましょう。

1.　　　　　　　　　　　　　　　CheckLink　DL008　CD1-08

Attention, _____ . This _____ will _____ at the final _____ at 2:30 P.M.

What is the topic of the announcement?
(A) Arrival time
(B) A form to complete
(C) A place to visit
(D) The departure gate

2.　　　　　　　　　　　　　　　CheckLink　DL009　CD1-09

_____ _____ the bad weather, the _____ to Manila will be _____.

What is being announced?
(A) A flight cancellation
(B) A mechanical problem
(C) A gate closure
(D) A flight delay

PART 5 短文穴埋め問題

品詞① 名詞
名詞は人や物の名前を表す語で、文の主語、目的語、補語になります。また、名詞には数えられる名詞（単数形・複数形）と数えられない名詞があります。なお、以下のように単語の語尾で名詞だとわかるものも多くあります。
-tion (information) / **-ment** (development) / **-ance** (importance) / **-ability** (availability)など

Practice!

x

概要に関する問題① 目的や概要は冒頭で述べられる

文書は、まず冒頭で目的や概要を述べてから詳細へと入っていくのが基本的な構造です。したがって、冒頭を読むことで「何について」の話かという情報がわかります。その上で、その後の展開を読むと理解しやすくなります。長文に苦手意識を持つ学習者は多いですが、この読み方ができるようになると、単語の意味が完全にはわからなくても内容を読み取れるようになります。

Practice!　　ⒸCheckLink　🎧DL016　◉CD1-13

文書を読んで、設問に対する最も適切な選択肢を選びましょう。その後で、正解の根拠となる部分にそれぞれ下線を引きましょう。

Dear Mr. Jackson,

Thank you for choosing Starshots Travels for your upcoming trip to Cebu. As you requested, a sightseeing tour has been added. Please take a look at the attached itinerary for details.

Please make a payment by October 10. After we have received your payment, we will send you flight tickets. Also, meal coupons for three people will be sent to you. You can use them upon your arrival at the hotel.

---

1. What is the purpose of the e-mail?
   (A) To apologize for some errors
   (B) To reply to some questions
   (C) To update information
   (D) To request feedback

2. What is attached to the e-mail?
   (A) Meal coupons
   (B) Boarding passes
   (C) A receipt of payment
   (D) A travel schedule

TOEIC
Mini Test

Select the one statement that best describes what you see in the picture.

1.

ⒶⒷⒸⒹ

2.

ⒶⒷⒸⒹ

Select the best response to the question or statement.

3. Mark your answer on your answer sheet.   ⒶⒷⒸ

4. Mark your answer on your answer sheet.   ⒶⒷⒸ

5. Mark your answer on your answer sheet.   ⒶⒷⒸ

6. Mark your answer on your answer sheet.   ⒶⒷⒸ

7. Mark your answer on your answer sheet.   ⒶⒷⒸ

8. Mark your answer on your answer sheet.   ⒶⒷⒸ

9. Mark your answer on your answer sheet.   ⒶⒷⒸ

PART 3

 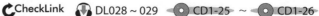

Select the best response to each question.

10. What are the speakers discussing?
    (A) The history of the city
    (B) A new itinerary
    (C) A guided tour
    (D) A reservation change

11. What does the woman give the man?
    (A) A receipt
    (B) A map
    (C) An itinerary
    (D) A voucher

12. What will the man probably do next?
    (A) Board a vehicle
    (B) Present a document
    (C) Have a meal
    (D) Fill out a form

PART 4

CheckLink DL028 ~ 029 CD1-25 ~ CD1-26

Select the best response to each question.

13. What is being announced?
    (A) The flight has been overbooked.
    (B) The weather is bad.
    (C) There has been a technical
        problem.
    (D) Some luggage has been lost.

14. What will be provided to some
listeners?
    (A) A ticket
    (B) A coupon
    (C) A form
    (D) A map

15. What should the listeners do at the
counter?
    (A) Ask for assistance
    (B) Make payment
    (C) Check in their luggage
    (D) Show some documents

Select the best answer to complete the sentence.

16. The travel agency sent an itinerary to Ms. Park after it confirmed -------.
(A) paying
(B) payment
(C) pays
(D) pay

17. Mr. Lopez will join some tours during his ------- in Singapore.
(A) will stay
(B) stayed
(C) stay
(D) to stay

18. If you need to change the number of people, please make a new -------.
(A) reserve
(B) reservation
(C) reserved
(D) reserving

19. When you book a -------, you can select either a window seat or an aisle seat.
(A) flight
(B) fly
(C) flies
(D) flying

20. You can check the ------- of the rooms at the hotel online.
(A) avail
(B) availably
(C) available
(D) availability

21. ------- of your reservation will be sent automatically after you complete the process.
(A) Confirmation
(B) Confirm
(C) Confirming
(D) Confirmed

22. According to Grand Travels, several sightseeing ------- will be added in two weeks.
(A) option
(B) optional
(C) optionally
(D) options

23. All the tours are already fully booked, but you can wait for a -------.
(A) cancel
(B) cancellation
(C) cancelled
(D) cancels

Select the best answer to complete the text.

Questions 24-27 refer to the following e-mail.

To: Lisa Hensley

From: KTS Travels

Date: April 9

Subject: Travel arrangement

Dear Ms. Hensley,

Thank you for choosing KTS Travels. Attached is your updated -------. It includes
                                                                          24.
flight and hotel information. There are several types of optional tours from one-
hour to one-day long. One-hour tours leave frequeutly. -------. If you wish to join
                                                                  25.
one or more of them, please let us know. We ------- their availability.
                                                      26.

If you have any questions about your -------, please contact us by e-mail or by
                                              27.
phone at 555-1129.

Sincerely,

KTS Travels

---

24. (A) departure
    (B) receipt
    (C) itinerary
    (D) coupon

25. (A) Unfortunately, they are fully
        booked.
    (B) We have received your payment.
    (C) You can board the vehicle at 9:00.
    (D) Please take a look at the
        pamphlet.

26. (A) checked
    (B) will check
    (C) checking
    (D) check

27. (A) reservation
    (B) feedback
    (C) luggage
    (D) arrival

Select the best answer for each question.

Questions 28-30 refer to the following e-mail.

To:	j.jackson@highlandmail.com
From:	Bartland Outdoors
Subject:	Re: Inquiry

Dear Ms. Jackson,

I am writing in response to your inquiry about our camp sites. We have selected several places that match your needs and budget. Please take a look at the attached digital documents. You can choose from various destinations, from mountain areas to riverside sites, both in the country and overseas. Equipment rentals are available for all of the listed areas. To feel the differences among the camp sites, please watch our videos at our Web site at www.bartlandoutdoors.com/camp_sites/videos.html.

If you have any questions, please do not hesitate to contact our service representative. Thank you very much for your interest.

Bartland Outdoors

28. What is the purpose of the e-mail?
(A) To change a reservation
(B) To reply to an inquiry
(C) To send an itinerary
(D) To request some documents

29. What is mentioned about the listed camp sites?
(A) Campers can rent some items.
(B) Discounts are offered for a limited period of time.
(C) They are located near Ms. Jackson's city.
(D) They are recommended for beginners.

30. According to the e-mail, what can people do on the Web site?
(A) Get a discount code
(B) Book a tour
(C) Order camping gear
(D) Watch some videos

TOEIC
Vocabularies & Phrases

Unit 2 Dining Out

次の Unit 2 に登場する TOEIC 頻出語句＆フレーズです。

Step 1	意味を確認した上で、音声に続いて音読してみましょう。
Step 2	再度音声を聞きながら、意味を思い出してみましょう。

🎧 DL040 ⊙ CD1-30

□□□ atmosphere	□□□ 名雰囲気
□□□ authentic	□□□ 形本物の、真の
□□□ bake	□□□ 動焼く
□□□ beverage	□□□ 名飲み物
□□□ catering	□□□ 名仕出し
□□□ comfortable	□□□ 形快適な
□□□ complimentary	□□□ 形無料の
□□□ cuisine	□□□ 名料理
□□□ diner	□□□ 名食事客
□□□ ingredient	□□□ 名材料、成分
□□□ meal	□□□ 名食事、食べ物
□□□ nutrition	□□□ 名栄養
□□□ prepare	□□□ 動準備する
□□□ reasonable	□□□ 形手ごろな
□□□ recipe	□□□ 名レシピ、料理法
□□□ refreshment	□□□ 名軽食
□□□ serve	□□□ 動給仕する、提供する
□□□ server	□□□ 名給仕係
□□□ taste	□□□ 名味　動味わう
□□□ traditional	□□□ 形伝統的な

Dining Out

学習目標
☐ 「食事」に関する語句・表現を覚える
☐ 形容詞を学ぶ

PART 1 写真描写問題

人物の動作② 2人のパターン
2人の人物の動作を表す文でも現在進行形が多く使われます。
　　Diners **are eating** at a restaurant.（食事客がレストランで食事をしている）
なお、2人の共通の動作またはどちらか片方の動作が描写される場合があります。主語がPeopleやDinersなどの場合は共通の動作、主語がOne of the men/womenやThe man/womanの場合は片方の人物の動作が描写されます。

Practice!　　　　　　CheckLink　　DL041　　CD1-31

音声を聞いて空所の語句を書き取り、写真を最も適切に表す選択肢を選びましょう。

(A) _____ are _____ at the _____.
(B) One of the men is _____　_____
　　　a _____.
(C) _____ are _____　_____
　　　_____.
(D) One of the men is _____ some _____.

PART 2 応答問題

WH疑問文② Whereで始まる疑問文
Whereは場所を問う疑問詞のため、応答は場所の名前になることが多くあります。また、「…の上」や「…の中」などの応答も頻出します。

Practice!　　CheckLink　　DL042〜043　　CD1-32　〜　CD1-33

音声を聞いて空所の語句を書き取り、最も適切な応答の選択肢を選びましょう。

1. Where can I _____ _____
Japanese food?
(A) At a _____ at the _____.
(B) I don't know _____
　　　_____ _____.
(C) I've _____ _____ to Japan.

2. Where did you _____ the _____?
(A) I _____ them _____.
(B) I _____ them in the _____.
(C) I don't _____ the _____.

PART 3 会話問題

会話が行われている場所を特定する

会話の冒頭を聞くことで、会話が行われている場所を特定することができます。restaurantやcatering companyなどの場所を表す語句がそのまま使われることもありますが、dinersやdeliver some refreshmentsなど、使われている語句から推測しなくてはいけない場合もあります。いずれにしても、冒頭を聞き逃さないように注意しましょう。

Practice!

音声を聞いて空所の語句を書き取り、設問に対する最も適切な選択肢を選びましょう。

1.　　　　　　　　　　　　　　　CheckLink 🎧 DL044 💿 CD1-34

M: We received an _____ for some _____ for 10 people.

W: Sure. Here, we have enough _____ for them, and there are

_____, too.

Where are the speakers?

(A) At a warehouse

(B) At a factory

(C) In a car

(D) In a kitchen

2.　　　　　　　　　　　　　　　CheckLink 🎧 DL045 💿 CD1-35

W: I really like this _____ _____ .

M: Thank you. We _____ _____ Hawaiian food and all of the

_____ come with a _____ dessert.

Where does the conversation most likely take place?

(A) At a supermarket

(B) At a bakery

(C) At a restaurant

(D) At a station

> **トークが行われている場所を特定する**
>
> Part 3と同様、冒頭でトークの「場所」が推測できるため、集中して聞きましょう。また、トークの中で使われている表現が、設問や選択肢では他の表現で言い換えられていることもあります。例えば、トーク内でsandwiches and drinksと言われたものが、選択肢ではrefreshmentsと言い換えられていたりするため、意味をよく理解して解答しましょう。

Practice!

音声を聞いて空所の語句を書き取り、設問に対する最も適切な選択肢を選びましょう。

1.   CheckLink   DL046   CD1-36

Attention, shoppers. We're now _____ _____, and it'll be ready in 10 minutes. Please enjoy our _____ flavors!

Where is the announcement most likely taking place?

(A) At a fruit shop

(B) At a bakery

(C) At a gift shop

(D) At a fish market

2.   CheckLink   DL047   CD1-37

As you can see, our _____ has been updated, and now it has information about _____ . As a _____, please be aware of this, and tell _____ about it at the table.

Where most likely are the listeners?

(A) At a catering company

(B) At a restaurant

(C) At a department store

(D) At a grocery store

PART 5 短文穴埋め問題

品詞② 形容詞

形容詞は**beautiful** flowerや**convenient** locationのように、名詞の状態や性質を説明します。なお、以下のように単語の語尾で形容詞だとわかるものも多くあります。

-tive (active) / **-ful** (successful) / **-ant** (important) / **-able** (reasonable) / **-ous** (famous) / **-al** (local)など

Practice!　　　　CheckLink　DL048 ~ 051　CD1-38

空所に入る正しい語句を選んで書き、文を完成させましょう。その後で、正解の根拠となる部分に下線を引きましょう。

1. Today's special comes with a _____ beverage.

(A) freely　　(B) free　　(C) freedom　　(D) frees

2. The new Japanese restaurant serves _____ cuisine.

(A) tradition　　(B) traditional　　(C) traditionally　　(D) traditions

3. The recipe was created by our _____ chef, Wayne Chang.

(A) famous　　(B) famously　　(C) fame　　(D) famousness

4. You can enjoy Mohan's authentic Indian food at _____ prices.

(A) reason　　(B) reasonably　　(C) reasonable　　(D) reasoning

PART 6 長文穴埋め問題

語彙問題② 難しめの語彙

Part 6の語彙問題には、難しめの単語が選択肢に並んでいることもあります。その場合、知っている単語が空所に入るかどうかを話の流れから確認していきましょう。また、消去法や推測も活用しながら解答しましょう。

Practice!　　　　CheckLink　DL052 ~ 053　　~　

空所に入る正しい語句を選んで書き、文書を完成させましょう。その後で、正解の根拠となる部分に下線を引きましょう。

---

1. Please note that the food order cannot be changed after October 10. However, you can add _____ until two days before the reservation date.

(A) atmosphere　　(B) beverages　　(C) nutrition　　(D) servers

---

2. The restaurant on the second floor serves _____ Japanese cuisine. Guests staying at our hotel can enjoy it at discounted prices.

(A) complimentary　　(B) authentic　　(C) tasting　　(D) dining

詳細情報に関する問題① 設問のキーワードを参考にする

設問が具体的な内容の場合、詳細な情報が問われています。設問にあるキーワードを参考に、本文から関連情報を探しましょう。例えば、When will the event be held? という設問の場合、「イベントの開催日」が問われています。イベントの開催に関する内容を文書から探し、該当箇所をしっかり読みます。日付や場所の場合は選択肢にそのまま書かれている場合が多いですが、内容によっては本文と選択肢で言い換えられている場合もあります。

Practice!

 CheckLink　DL054　CD1-41

文書を読んで、設問に対する最も適切な選択肢を選びましょう。その後で、正解の根拠となる部分にそれぞれ下線を引きましょう。

Roberto's Trattoria to Open in Springfield!
188 Stone Avenue

This world-famous Italian restaurant is finally coming to Springfield on October 22! Originally from Italy, Roberto's Trattoria has opened in more than 10 countries, with 20 branches in the U.S. We serve authentic Italian cuisine with traditional ingredients. The head chef has experience working in Italy for more than 5 years, and has his own original recipes that you have never tasted before.

The restaurant will be open from 11:00 A.M. to 9:00 P.M., from Tuesday through Sunday. Reservations are available through our Web site at www.robertostrattoria. com. Until the end of the year, all dishes come with a complimentary beverage.

---

1. How can diners book a table at Roberto's Trattoria?

 (A) By going online

 (B) By making a phone call

 (C) By sending an e-mail

 (D) By returning a form

2. What is the limited offer?

 (A) A coupon

 (B) A complimentary mug

 (C) A free drink

 (D) A membership card

TOEIC
Mini Test

PART 1

CheckLink DL055 ~ 056 CD1-42 ~ CD1-43

Select the one statement that best describes what you see in the picture.

1.

Ⓐ Ⓑ Ⓒ Ⓓ

2.

Ⓐ Ⓑ Ⓒ Ⓓ

PART 2

CheckLink DL057 ~ 063 CD1-44 ~ CD1-50

Select the best response to the question or statement.

3. Mark your answer on your answer sheet.   Ⓐ Ⓑ Ⓒ

4. Mark your answer on your answer sheet.   Ⓐ Ⓑ Ⓒ

5. Mark your answer on your answer sheet.   Ⓐ Ⓑ Ⓒ

6. Mark your answer on your answer sheet.   Ⓐ Ⓑ Ⓒ

7. Mark your answer on your answer sheet.   Ⓐ Ⓑ Ⓒ

8. Mark your answer on your answer sheet.   Ⓐ Ⓑ Ⓒ

9. Mark your answer on your answer sheet.   Ⓐ Ⓑ Ⓒ

PART 3

CheckLink DL064 ~ 065 CD1-51 ~ CD1-52

Select the best response to each question.

10. Where does the conversation most
likely take place?
(A) At a beverage company
(B) At a catering company
(C) At a cafeteria
(D) At a food market

11. What does the woman ask about?
(A) The number of people
(B) The time
(C) The method of payment
(D) Drinks

12. What did BS Technologies like
before?
(A) The price
(B) The location
(C) The food variety
(D) The operation

PART 4

CheckLink DL066 ~ 067 CD1-53 ~ CD1-54

Select the best response to each question.

13. Where is the talk most likely taking
place?
(A) On the radio
(B) At a restaurant
(C) On an airplane
(D) At an event

14. Why would the listeners visit the Web
site?
(A) To book a table
(B) To write a review
(C) To see some information
(D) To send some photos

15. What is offered to the listeners?
(A) A postcard
(B) A complimentary drink
(C) A discount
(D) A map around the area

Select the best answer to complete the sentence.

16. We serve dishes with ------- ingredients.
    (A) nutritiously
    (B) nutrition
    (C) nutritionist
    (D) nutritious

17. The old Japanese restaurant is famous for serving ------- dishes.
    (A) tradition
    (B) traditionally
    (C) traditions
    (D) traditional

18. The recipe shows how to prepare ------- coffee at home.
    (A) tasty
    (B) taste
    (C) tasting
    (D) tastes

19. Our company cafeteria has a ------- atmosphere.
    (A) comfortable
    (B) comfortably
    (C) comfort
    (D) comfortability

20. The second store of Grand Dining will open near a ------- place.
    (A) history
    (B) historical
    (C) historically
    (D) histories

21. Murton's Bistro serves all of its food at ------- prices
    (A) lowness
    (B) lowly
    (C) lowering
    (D) low

22. Enns Café received ------- reviews from local customers.
    (A) positiveness
    (B) positivity
    (C) positive
    (D) positively

23. We cater ------- Italian meals to any event from small to large.
    (A) authentically
    (B) authentic
    (C) authenticity
    (D) authenticate

PART 6

Select the best answer to complete the text.

Questions 24-27 refer to the following notice.

To: All employees

This is to inform you that a new recipe tasting will take place for three days next
month. It will be held on May 8, 9, and 10 at the company cafeteria. One ------- **24.**
dish will be served each day. Our chef will talk about nutrition. -------. If you are **25.**
interested in attending the tasting, please send an e-mail to Ronald Sasaki ------- **26.**
April 20. We look forward to serving many more nutritious dishes to our -------. **27.**

---

24. (A) operational
    (B) valid
    (C) complimentary
    (D) following

25. (A) You can eat traditional food at a
        reasonable price.
    (B) Participants are asked to fill out a
        survey.
    (C) Thank you for your application.
    (D) It will be delivered to your office.

26. (A) with
    (B) in
    (C) at
    (D) by

27. (A) employees
    (B) chefs
    (C) refreshments
    (D) beverages

Select the best answer for each question.

Questions 28-30 refer to the following advertisement.

Olive Street Catering Company

Over the years, Olive Street Catering Company has been serving the Metro region. We cater a wide variety of events from small weddings to large celebrations according to your needs and budget. Our experienced chefs prepare authentic Italian food, and it is delivered fresh from the kitchen! A vegetarian option is available.

Visit our Web site at www.olivestreetcateringcompany.com to check our special menu. Also, you can read positive reviews from our customers. There are many companies who hire us for every event they plan.

A tasting is scheduled for September 1 at our headquarters. If you are interested in tasting our food at a reasonable price, just book a table through the Web site.

---

28. What does Olive Street Catering Company offer?
(A) Complimentary beverages
(B) A membership discount
(C) A meal option
(D) Delivery to far places

29. What is available at the Web site?
(A) A discount coupon
(B) Information about nutrition
(C) A map of the region
(D) Customer feedback

30. What will take place on September 1?
(A) A food tasting
(B) The opening of a new branch
(C) A Web site update
(D) A cooking workshop

TOEIC
Vocabularies & Phrases

Unit 3　Daily Life

次の Unit 3 に登場する TOEIC 頻出語句＆フレーズです。

> **Step 1**　意味を確認した上で、音声に続いて音読してみましょう。
> **Step 2**　再度音声を聞きながら、意味を思い出してみましょう。

🎧 DL078　💿 CD1-58

☐☐☐ adjust	☐☐☐ 動調節する
☐☐☐ appliance	☐☐☐ 名（電気）器具、電化製品
☐☐☐ be located	☐☐☐ ……に位置する
☐☐☐ checkup	☐☐☐ 名健康診断
☐☐☐ detour	☐☐☐ 名回り道　動迂回する
☐☐☐ electricity	☐☐☐ 名電気
☐☐☐ equipment	☐☐☐ 名機器
☐☐☐ maintain	☐☐☐ 動維持する
☐☐☐ mayor	☐☐☐ 名市長
☐☐☐ neighborhood	☐☐☐ 名近所、地域
☐☐☐ pharmacy	☐☐☐ 名薬局
☐☐☐ plant	☐☐☐ 名植物、工場　動植える
☐☐☐ plumber	☐☐☐ 名配管工
☐☐☐ property	☐☐☐ 名不動産、所有物
☐☐☐ real estate	☐☐☐ 名不動産
☐☐☐ renovate	☐☐☐ 動改修する、修復する
☐☐☐ rent	☐☐☐ 名家賃
	動（お金を払って）借りる、貸す
☐☐☐ repair	☐☐☐ 名修理　動修理する
☐☐☐ resident	☐☐☐ 名住民
☐☐☐ transportation	☐☐☐ 名交通機関、輸送

Unit 3 Daily Life

学習目標
☐ 「日常生活」に関する語句・表現を覚える
☐ 副詞を学ぶ

PART 1 写真描写問題

人物の動作③ 3人以上のパターン

3人以上が写っている場合、全員に共通する動作や人物がいる場所が描写されます。

People are entering a building. (人々が建物の中に入っていくところである)

なお、1人だけ他と異なる動作をしている場合、その1人が描写される場合もあります。

Practice!  CheckLink DL079 CD1-59

音声を聞いて空所の語句を書き取り、写真を最も適切に表す選択肢を選びましょう。

(A) People are _____ some _____.

(B) A woman is _____ _____.

(C) A man is _____ _____.

(D) People are _____ in _____ of some _____.

PART 2 応答問題

WH疑問文③ Whenで始まる疑問文

Whenは時を問う疑問詞のため、応答は時を表す表現であることが多くあります。聞かれているのが過去のことなのか未来のことなのかも、しっかりと聞き取りましょう。

Practice! CheckLink DL080～081 CD1-60 ～ CD1-61

音声を聞いて空所の語句を書き取り、最も適切な応答の選択肢を選びましょう。

1. When is your _____ _____ scheduled for?

   (A) _____ a _____.

   (B) At a _____ _____.

   (C) _____ _____.

2. When did you _____ the _____?

   (A) With the _____ _____ _____.

   (B) Before I _____ to the _____.

   (C) The _____ _____ is high.

PART 3 会話問題

Practice!

音声を聞いて空所の語句を書き取り、設問に対する最も適切な選択肢を選びましょう。

1.　　　　　　　　　　　　　　CheckLink　DL082　CD1-62

M: Hi, I saw an _____ and I'd like to _____ the _____ on Elm Street.

W: Thank you for calling. It's _____ in a _____ _____. When would you like to _____?

Where does the woman probably work?

(A) At a dentist

(B) At an appliance store

(C) At a real estate agency

(D) At a furniture store

2.　　　　　　　　　　　　　　CheckLink　DL083　CD1-63

W: Hello, there's a _____ with the _____ in my _____, and I'd like you to _____ it as soon as possible.

M: Let me check the _____ of our _____.

What kind of business does the man work for?

(A) A vehicle repair shop

(B) A plumbing company

(C) A pharmacy

(D) A hair salon

PART 4 説明文問題

トークから話し手の働いている場所や部門を推測する

Part 3と同様、トークの話し手の職業や勤務先が問われることがあります。その場合、冒頭部分の内容を聞き取ることで、場所や部門を把握することができます。トーク内の表現が選択肢では言い換えられることもあるため、内容を関連付けることも求められます。

Practice!

音声を聞いて空所の語句を書き取り、設問に対する最も適切な選択肢を選びましょう。

1.　　　　　　　　　　　　　　　　ⓒCheckLink　🎧 DL084　◎ CD1-64

Hello, Mr. Lopez. This is Anne Smith from Dr. Lee's office. I'm calling to _____ _____ _____ that it's time for your _____ _____ . It's important to _____ _____ _____ to enjoy your daily life. To schedule an _____, please call us at 555-0112.

Where does the speaker probably work?
(A) At an appliance store
(B) At a grocery store
(C) At a dentist
(D) At a station

2.　　　　　　　　　　　　　　　　ⓒCheckLink　🎧 DL085　◎ CD1-65

Hello, listeners. The _____ has announced that the _____ plans to _____ the West Bridge. _____ going to Stanton are required to _____ a _____. The work is scheduled to be completed in two weeks.

Where does the speaker most likely work?
(A) At a real estate agency
(B) At a hotel
(C) At a radio station
(D) At a plumbing company

PART 5 短文穴埋め問題

品詞③ 副詞
副詞は be **strongly** recommended や **internationally** famous のように、主に名詞以外の動詞や形容詞を説明します。副詞のほとんどは語尾が ly で終わるため、判断しやすいでしょう。また、以下のように副詞から ly を取り除くと形容詞になります。
successfully → successful　productively → productive

Practice!
CheckLink　DL086 ~ 089　CD1-66

空所に入る正しい語句を選んで書き、文を完成させましょう。その後で、正解の根拠となる部分に下線を引きましょう。

1. It is _____ important to use less electricity to save costs.
   (A) high　(B) highly　(C) height　(D) heighten

2. The apartment building is _____ located in a quiet neighborhood.
   (A) convenience　(B) convenient　(C) conveniences　(D) conveniently

3. The appliance is still new, but it breaks down _____.
   (A) frequently　(B) frequency　(C) frequent　(D) frequencies

4. Please read the manual to adjust the dial _____.
   (A) correction　(B) correctly　(C) correct　(D) correctness

PART 6 長文穴埋め問題

語彙問題③ まとめ
Part 6 の語彙問題では、空所の前後や空所を含む文を読んだだけでは解けないものが多くあります。やさしめの語彙・難しめの語彙にかかわらず、空所を含む文だけで解けない場合は、前後の文脈を関連付けて正確に理解するようにしましょう。

Practice!
CheckLink　DL090 ~ 091　CD1-67　~　CD1-68

空所に入る正しい語句を選んで書き、文書を完成させましょう。その後で、正解の根拠となる部分に下線を引きましょう。

1. Before moving into the apartment, please sign a form to start using _____.
   As soon as we receive it, you can turn on the lights.

(A) water　(B) furniture　(C) neighborhood　(D) electricity

2. The city hall has a long history, and it's getting old. Therefore, the mayor plans to _____ the whole building.

(A) renovate　(B) adjust　(C) rent　(D) visit

PART 7 読解問題

推測させる問題① キーワードを参考に情報を読み取る

What is indicated about the new product?（新製品について何が示されていますか）やWhat is mentioned about Mr. Jackson?（ジャクソンさんについて何が述べられていますか）のように設問が抽象的な場合、具体的な情報を読み取るのではなく、本文の深い理解が問われています。aboutの後ろのキーワードを参考にして情報を読み取りましょう。多くの場合、本文の語句と選択肢の語句は言い換えられています。

Practice!

CheckLink   DL092   CD1-69

文書を読んで、設問に対する最も適切な選択肢を選びましょう。その後で、正解の根拠となる部分にそれぞれ下線を引きましょう。

Dear Mr. Trevor,

Thank you for your e-mail, and I am writing to answer your questions about our repair service. We offer quick repairs for everything from digital devices and home appliances to wooden and metal furniture. Also, we can maintain equipment so that it continues to work smoothly.

Our shop is located next to Goose Park, with easy access from public transportation. We offer a discount to first-time customers until the end of the month. Just use the discount code TRS105012 when you apply.

If you have any other questions, please don't hesitate to ask us.

Best regards,
Cecil Anderson, Tyron's Repair Shop

1. What is indicated about Mr. Trevor?
   (A) He repairs home appliances.
   (B) He lives near Goose Park.
   (C) He bought some equipment a long time ago.
   (D) He sent an e-mail to Tyron's Repair Shop.

2. What is indicated about the discount?
   (A) It can be used for two more months.
   (B) It is available for city residents.
   (C) It is offered to new customers.
   (D) It cannot be used for maintenance.

TOEIC
Mini Test

PART 1

CheckLink   DL093 ~ 094   CD1-70 ~ CD1-71

Select the one statement that best describes what you see in the picture.

1.

Ⓐ Ⓑ Ⓒ Ⓓ

2.

Ⓐ Ⓑ Ⓒ Ⓓ

PART 2

CheckLink   DL095 ~ 101   CD1-72 ~ CD1-78

Select the best response to the question or statement.

3. Mark your answer on your answer sheet.   Ⓐ Ⓑ Ⓒ

4. Mark your answer on your answer sheet.   Ⓐ Ⓑ Ⓒ

5. Mark your answer on your answer sheet.   Ⓐ Ⓑ Ⓒ

6. Mark your answer on your answer sheet.   Ⓐ Ⓑ Ⓒ

7. Mark your answer on your answer sheet.   Ⓐ Ⓑ Ⓒ

8. Mark your answer on your answer sheet.   Ⓐ Ⓑ Ⓒ

9. Mark your answer on your answer sheet.   Ⓐ Ⓑ Ⓒ

PART 3

CheckLink DL102 ~ 103 CD1-79 ~ CD1-80

Select the best response to each question.

10. Where does the woman work?
   (A) At a dental clinic
   (B) At a pharmacy
   (C) At a real estate agency
   (D) At a restaurant

11. What does the man plan to do?
   (A) View a property
   (B) Work overtime
   (C) Have a checkup
   (D) Reschedule a meeting

12. What does the woman say about noon?
   (A) It is a busy time.
   (B) The office will be closed.
   (C) It is already booked.
   (D) Electricity will be off.

PART 4

CheckLink DL104 ~ 105 CD1-81 ~ CD1-82

Select the best response to each question.

13. What kind of business does the speaker probably work for?
   (A) A dentist
   (B) A repair shop
   (C) An appliance store
   (D) A delivery company

14. What is the problem?
   (A) The wrong product has arrived.
   (B) Delivery cannot be completed.
   (C) Payment has not been received.
   (D) A machine cannot be adjusted.

15. What will the speaker do in the evening?
   (A) Contact the listener
   (B) Repair a machine
   (C) Return to the building
   (D) Cancel the order

Select the best answer to complete the sentence.

16. A plumber will arrive at the apartment -------.
(A) short
(B) shortness
(C) shortly
(D) shorten

17. The mayor recommends that residents use public transportation -------.
(A) regular
(B) regulate
(C) regularization
(D) regularly

18. The detour sign is ------- marked on Brown Street.
(A) clear
(B) clearness
(C) clearly
(D) cleared

19. Ms. Moore called a plumber to repair the sink -------.
(A) quick
(B) quicken
(C) quickly
(D) quickness

20. After the renovation, the apartment lobby looks ------- different.
(A) complete
(B) completely
(C) completion
(D) completed

21. Before using the equipment, please adjust it -------.
(A) carefully
(B) carefulness
(C) careful
(D) care

22. You should maintain the furniture ------- to keep a good condition.
(A) periodical
(B) periods
(C) period
(D) periodically

23. Most of the comments from our customers show that our plumbers provide ------- professional services.
(A) high
(B) highness
(C) highly
(D) height

PART 6

Select the best answer to complete the text.

Questions 24-27 refer to the following notice.

From: Mayor

To: City residents

This is to inform you that Grayson Street is scheduled for repair work in
September. The ------- includes some road repairs and planting trees along the
      24.
city parking lot. -------. There may be some ------- caused by the work.
    25.   **26.**
Also, electricity may be off for a few hours in some areas. ------- about this will
              27.
be provided at a later date. If you have any questions, please contact the city
office at 555-0249. We apologize for any inconvenience this may cause.

---

24. (A) move
    (B) work
    (C) policy
    (D) delay

25. (A) Please bring your driver's license.
    (B) The monthly rent will increase.
    (C) It will be located in our
        neighborhood.
    (D) It will take two weeks.

26. (A) transportation
    (B) noise
    (C) community
    (D) preparation

27. (A) Informatively
    (B) Informative
    (C) Inform
    (D) Information

Select the best answer for each question.

Questions 28-30 refer to the following e-mail.

To:	Hannah Manning
From:	Lily Real Estate
Date:	April 28
Subject:	Apartment

Dear Ms. Manning,

I am writing to inform you that we have found an apartment that you might be interested in renting. Although it is farther from the office than the apartment we showed you last week, it is located in a quiet neighborhood in Jacksonville, with easy access to public transportation.

The apartment has two bedrooms and is fully furnished. You can enjoy Swedish furniture and compact appliances including a refrigerator and washing machine. Also, the stylish kitchen was renovated only two months ago. You can park your car in the garage.

For more information about this property or other properties, together with photos, please visit our Web site at www.lilyrealestate.com. Property viewing is available, but the apartment won't last long, so I recommend you act quickly.

Best regards,
Madison Dowie, Lily Real Estate

28. What is indicated about the apartment in Jacksonville?

(A) It is on the top floor.

(B) It is equipped with furniture.

(C) It is located near the office.

(D) It requires repairs.

29. What is mentioned about the kitchen?

(A) It is spacious.

(B) It was designed by a famous chef.

(C) It has a dishwasher.

(D) It is newly renovated.

30. Why should Ms. Manning visit the Web site?

(A) To apply for membership

(B) To find a map to the real estate agency

(C) To see some images

(D) To recommend a friend

TOEIC
Vocabularies & Phrases

Unit 4　Entertainment

次の Unit 4 に登場する TOEIC 頻出語句＆フレーズです。

| Step 1 | 意味を確認した上で、音声に続いて音読してみましょう。 |
| Step 2 | 再度音声を聞きながら、意味を思い出してみましょう。 |

🎧 DL116　💿 CD2-02

□□□ actor / actress	□□□ 名俳優／女優
□□□ admission	□□□ 名入場（料）
□□□ audience	□□□ 名観客、聴衆
□□□ award-winning	□□□ 形受賞した、受賞経験のある
□□□ box office	□□□ チケット売り場
□□□ excited	□□□ 形興奮した
□□□ exhibition	□□□ 名展示会、展示（物）
□□□ fee	□□□ 名料金、入場料
□□□ hang	□□□ 動吊るす、掛ける、掛かる
□□□ instrument	□□□ 名楽器、道具
□□□ novel	□□□ 名小説
□□□ outstanding	□□□ 形卓越した
□□□ performance	□□□ 名演技、公演、業績
□□□ pile up	□□□ 動積み重ねる
□□□ publisher	□□□ 名出版社
□□□ reputation	□□□ 名評判
□□□ review	□□□ 名批評、再検討
	動 批評する、再検討する
□□□ role	□□□ 名役、役割
□□□ souvenir	□□□ 名おみやげ、記念品
□□□ spectator	□□□ 名観客

Unit 4 Entertainment

学習目標
- ☐ 「娯楽」に関する語句・表現を覚える
- ☐ 代名詞を学ぶ

PART 1 写真描写問題

光景① 受動態が使われるパターン

物が主語の場合、描写の多くは受動態が用いられます。

Some boxes **are piled up**.（箱が積み重ねられている）

主語である物が、その動作を受けた状態かどうかを確認しながら解答しましょう。

Practice!  CheckLink 🎧 DL117 ◎ CD2-03

音声を聞いて空所の語句を書き取り、写真を最も適切に表す選択肢を選びましょう。

(A) Books are _____ on _____.

(B) Furniture is _____ in the _____ of
the _____.

(C) Books are _____ _____ on
the _____.

(D) Paintings are _____ on the _____.

PART 2 応答問題

WH疑問文④ Whyで始まる疑問文

Whyは理由を問う疑問詞です。正しい応答を選ぶには、疑問詞Whyの聞き取りだけでなく、内容の理解が求められます。また、WhenやWhereで始まる疑問文の応答とは異なり、TomorrowやAt the post officeのようにひと言で答えることはできないため、応答の意味も正確に理解する必要があります。

Practice! CheckLink 🎧 DL118 ～ 119 ◎ CD2-04 ～ ◎ CD2-05

音声を聞いて空所の語句を書き取り、最も適切な応答の選択肢を選びましょう。

1. Why did you _____ the _____?

  (A) _____ _____ by _____.

  (B) _____ a new _____ has _____.

  (C) At the _____ _____.

2. Why is the _____ _____?

  (A) It was an _____ _____.

  (B) I _____ a _____.

  (C) To attract a _____ _____.

会話内の質問・依頼を聞き取る

会話内での質問や依頼の内容に関する設問は頻繁に出題されます。設問に、What does the woman ask about?（女性は何について尋ねていますか）やWhat does the man ask the woman to do?（男性は女性に何をするよう求めていますか）などがある場合は、それらの内容をピンポイントで聞き取ることが求められます。依頼の場合は、Could you ...?（…していただけますか）やPlease ...（…してください）などの表現もヒントとなります。

Practice!

音声を聞いて空所の語句を書き取り、設問に対する最も適切な選択肢を選びましょう。

1.　　　　　　　　　　　　　　　ＣCheckLink　　DL120　　CD2-06

W: Do you know ＿＿＿＿＿＿＿ the ＿＿＿＿＿＿＿ is on the ＿＿＿＿＿＿＿?

M: Yes, he's James Affleck. He has a good ＿＿＿＿＿＿＿ for his ＿＿＿＿＿＿＿.

What does the woman ask about?

(A) The price of admission

(B) The name of an actor

(C) The location of an event

(D) The title of a novel

2.　　　　　　　　　　　　　　　ＣCheckLink　　DL121　　CD2-07

W: I've just finished ＿＿＿＿＿＿＿ a new ＿＿＿＿＿＿＿ by an ＿＿＿＿＿＿＿ writer, Hugh Hansen.

M: ＿＿＿＿＿＿＿ ＿＿＿＿＿＿＿ write a ＿＿＿＿＿＿＿ ＿＿＿＿＿＿＿ for the next ＿＿＿＿＿＿＿ on our blog?

What does the man ask the woman to do?

(A) Contact a publisher

(B) Invite an actor

(C) Post a review

(D) Change a role

PART 4 説明文問題

トーク内の質問・依頼を聞き取る

Part 3と同様に、Part 4でも質問や依頼に関する問題が出題されます。設問には、**What does the speaker ask the listeners to do?**（話し手は聞き手に何をするよう求めていますか）という話し手が主語のもののほかに、**What are the listeners asked to do?**（聞き手は何をするよう求められていますか）のように聞き手が主語のものがあります。

Practice!

CheckLink DL122 CD2-08

音声を聞いて空所の語句を書き取り、設問に対する最も適切な選択肢を選びましょう。

1.

Welcome to National Museum of Art. Before we begin our _____, please _____ _____ your _____ _____. You are not _____ to take _____ of any _____.

What does the speaker ask the listeners to do?

(A) Pay an admission fee
(B) Show their photo identification
(C) Look at souvenirs
(D) Switch off a device

2.

CheckLink DL123 CD2-09

_____ for the contest is almost complete. Now, _____ are _____ _____ on the table, so please _____ _____ _____ on the _____.

What are the listeners asked to do?

(A) Arrange tables
(B) Hang paintings on the wall
(C) Review photos
(D) Get ready for a performance

PART 5 短文穴埋め問題

代名詞

代名詞とは、名詞の代わりに使われるものです。Part 5では、異なる格同士（I/my/me/mineなど）か同じ格同士（I/you/he/she/it/we/theyなど）の使い方が問われます。IとYou以外の代名詞は、すでに出てきた人物や内容を指す際に用いられるため、何を指しているかを読み取る力も求められます。

Practice!   CheckLink   DL124 ~ 127   CD2-10

空所に入る正しい語句を選んで書き、文を完成させましょう。その後で、正解の根拠となる部分に下線を引きましょう。

1. Please do not leave _____ personal items in the museum lobby.

(A) your   (B) you   (C) yourself   (D) yours

2. Spectators were excited because _____ enjoyed the outstanding performance.

(A) their   (B) them   (C) themselves   (D) they

3. Patricia Shill received positive reviews from _____ readers.

(A) its   (B) their   (C) her   (D) that

4. If you have any questions about admission, please contact _____ by e-mail.

(A) you   (B) us   (C) it   (D) them

PART 6 長文穴埋め問題

代名詞① 主格（I / you / he / she / it / they）

代名詞に関する問題は、前の文を参考にして「誰」または「何」のことを指しているかを読み取ることが必要です。前後の文脈を関連付けて、正確に理解するようにしましょう。

Practice!   CheckLink   DL128 ~ 129   CD2-11 ~ CD2-12

空所に入る正しい語句を選んで書き、文書を完成させましょう。その後で、正解の根拠となる部分に下線を引きましょう。

1. The audience enjoyed the award-winning musician's performance. _____ played several musical instruments.

(A) He   (B) We   (C) It   (D) You

2. Jasmine Redmond has a good reputation as a young actress. The producer of the musical, *Under the Sea*, announced that _____ has been selected to play the lead role.

(A) they   (B) she   (C) I   (D) it

Unit 4 **Entertainment**   53

PART 7 読解問題

Practice!  CheckLink DL130 CD2-13

文書を読んで、設問に対する最も適切な選択肢を選びましょう。その後で、正解の根拠と
なる部分にそれぞれ下線を引きましょう。

The Venus Museum will start a new exhibition on August 12. It features historical paintings, wooden toys from all over the world, and photos by local artists. Also, new items such as photos and posters are available at our gift shop.

The admission fee is 8 dollars for adults, and 4 dollars for children aged 12 or under. A membership discount is available, so if you are a member, please do not forget to bring your membership card.

---

1. What is NOT one of the features of the new exhibition?
   (A) Toys
   (B) Photos
   (C) Paintings
   (D) Music

2. What is mentioned in the advertisement?
   (A) A new museum will open.
   (B) A building has been renovated.
   (C) A discount will be offered.
   (D) Admission will be free of charge.

TOEIC
Mini Test

PART 1

CheckLink   DL131 ~ 132   CD2-14 ~ CD2-15

Select the one statement that best describes what you see in the picture.

1.

Ⓐ Ⓑ Ⓒ Ⓓ

2.

Ⓐ Ⓑ Ⓒ Ⓓ

PART 2

CheckLink   DL133 ~ 139   CD2-16 ~ CD2-22

Select the best response to the question or statement.

3. Mark your answer on your answer sheet.   Ⓐ Ⓑ Ⓒ

4. Mark your answer on your answer sheet.   Ⓐ Ⓑ Ⓒ

5. Mark your answer on your answer sheet.   Ⓐ Ⓑ Ⓒ

6. Mark your answer on your answer sheet.   Ⓐ Ⓑ Ⓒ

7. Mark your answer on your answer sheet.   Ⓐ Ⓑ Ⓒ

8. Mark your answer on your answer sheet.   Ⓐ Ⓑ Ⓒ

9. Mark your answer on your answer sheet.   Ⓐ Ⓑ Ⓒ

PART 3

CheckLink DL140 ~ 141 CD2-23 ~ CD2-24

Select the best response to each question.

10. What are the speakers mainly
discussing?
(A) A movie
(B) A music concert
(C) An art exhibition
(D) A theatrical performance

11. What does the woman ask the man
to do?
(A) Wait for her answer
(B) Go to the box office
(C) Pay fees online
(D) Bring a document

12. Who most likely is Jose Alcantara?
(A) A famous novelist
(B) A magazine writer
(C) An outstanding actor
(D) An award-winning artist

PART 4

CheckLink  DL142 ~ 143 CD2-25 ~ CD2-26

Select the best response to each question.

13. What is the broadcast mainly about?
(A) A weather update
(B) A personal story
(C) Business news
(D) An upcoming project

14. Why does the speaker provide an
e-mail address?
(A) To ask for area information
(B) To conduct a survey
(C) To receive questions
(D) To collect reviews

15. What does the speaker ask about?
(A) The name of an athlete
(B) The location of a building
(C) The schedule for the next phase
(D) The beginning of a career

PART 5

Select the best answer to complete the sentence.

16. Ken Young has a good reputation for
------- outstanding performances.
(A) he
(B) his
(C) him
(D) himself

17. The publisher received book reviews,
and put ------- on the Web site.
(A) they
(B) their
(C) them
(D) theirs

18. The theme park plans to build a new
attraction, and ------- will play an
important role.
(A) he
(B) his
(C) its
(D) it

19. Spectators were excited about the
victory of ------- favorite team.
(A) their
(B) its
(C) his
(D) her

20. Do not pile up musical instruments
because ------- break easily.
(A) you
(B) we
(C) it
(D) they

21. An award-winning writer will talk
about ------- new novel next Monday.
(A) her
(B) hers
(C) she
(D) herself

22. Before you hang up the paintings,
please arrange ------- in the correct
order.
(A) us
(B) it
(C) them
(D) you

23. Please take your ticket with ------- to
receive a discount on souvenirs.
(A) yourself
(B) you
(C) yours
(D) your

PART 6

Select the best answer to complete the text.

Questions 24-27 refer to the following advertisement.

When you were a little child, didn't you ever dream of singing or acting on a big stage? -------. Your kids may feel the same. Hilltown Hall will make your kids'
      24.

dream come ------- at the Great Experience Event from November 4 to 6. We will
      25.

invite professional actors and musicians as instructors. ------- will teach kids how
      26.

to sing and act. To learn more about this -------, please visit our Web site at
      27.

www.hilltownhall.com.

---

24. (A) It will be smaller than that.
    (B) He is an award-winning actor.
    (C) It was an outstanding
        performance.
    (D) Yes, we all did.

25. (A) true
    (B) complete
    (C) again
    (D) excited

26. (A) You
    (B) I
    (C) They
    (D) She

27. (A) policy
    (B) event
    (C) system
    (D) location

PART 7

Select the best answer for each question.

Questions 28-30 refer to the following advertisement.

The Gaston Museum has had a great reputation for exhibitions over the years. We will mark the 60th anniversary this year, and have a lecture by Naomi Wharton, a professor of art history at the University of South Florida on February 13. At the reception in the evening, we will have a classic concert by an award-winning group, the Anthony Orchestra. Everyone will receive a pen, a small bag, and a voucher that you can use at our souvenir shop. The admission fee is $15 for adults, and $8 for children. Payment can be made online. For more information, please visit our Web site at www. gastonmuseum.com.

---

28. What is the purpose of the event?
(A) To announce new exhibitions
(B) To congratulate local musicians
(C) To celebrate an anniversary
(D) To give awards to artists

29. What will NOT be offered to the audience?
(A) A writing tool
(B) A complimentary snack
(C) A bag
(D) A coupon

30. What is indicated about the admission fee?
(A) It can be paid online.
(B) It will be discounted.
(C) It is the same for adults and children.
(D) It has been changed.

TOEIC
Vocabularies & Phrases

Unit 5 Purchasing

次のUnit 5に登場するTOEIC頻出語句＆フレーズです。

Step 1	意味を確認した上で、音声に続いて音読してみましょう。
Step 2	再度音声を聞きながら、意味を思い出してみましょう。

🎧 DL154 ⏺ CD2-30

□□□ cashier		名レジ係、会計係
□□□ customer		名客
□□□ exchange		動交換する
□□□ expire		動期限が切れる
□□□ function		名機能　動機能する
□□□ guarantee		名保証（書）　動保証する
□□□ item		名商品、品物
□□□ order form		注文書、注文用紙
□□□ out of stock		在庫切れ
□□□ purchase		名購入　動購入する
□□□ receipt		名領収書、レシート
□□□ refund		名払い戻し、返金　動払い戻す
□□□ replace		動取り替える、交換する
□□□ satisfaction		名満足
□□□ shipping		名発送、出荷、配送
□□□ shop clerk		店員
□□□ try on		試着する
□□□ valid		形有効な
□□□ various		形さまざまな
□□□ warranty		名保証（書）

Purchasing

PART 1 写真描写問題

人物の位置・場所① 1人のパターン

人物の位置関係が描写される際には、前置詞がポイントです。

The woman is standing **near** a bookshelf. (女性が本棚の近くに立っている)

in front of ... (…の前に)、behind ... (…の後ろに)、next to ... (…の隣に) など、位置関係が適切かどうかを確認しましょう。また、いる場所が明らかな場合には、in the parkやin the libraryのように描写されることもあります。

Practice! ↻CheckLink 🎧 DL155 ⊙ CD2-31

音声を聞いて空所の語句を書き取り、写真を最も適切に表す選択肢を選びましょう。

(A) The man is _____ _____
   _____ a _____.
(B) The man is _____ _____
   the _____.
(C) The man is _____ _____
   a _____.
(D) The man is _____ _____
   _____ the _____.

PART 2 応答問題

WH疑問文⑤ Howで始まる疑問文

Howは、How did you order lunch? (どうやって昼食を注文しましたか) のような「手段」だけでなく、How's your new job? (新しい仕事はどうですか) のように「状況」を尋ねることもできます。正しい応答を選ぶためには、どちらの意味なのかを正確に理解することが求められます。

Practice! ↻CheckLink 🎧 DL156～157 ⊙ CD2-32 ～ ⊙ CD2-33

音声を聞いて空所の語句を書き取り、最も適切な応答の選択肢を選びましょう。

1. How can I _____ a _____?
   (A) For a _____ _____.
   (B) It's _____ _____ _____.
   (C) Just _____ _____ the counter.

2. How's your _____ _____?
   (A) It has _____ _____.
   (B) I'd like to _____ it.
   (C) It will _____ _____.

PART 3 会話問題

Practice!

音声を聞いて空所の語句を書き取り、設問に対する最も適切な選択肢を選びましょう。

1. CheckLink DL158 CD2-34

M: I _____ this _____ yesterday, but it's too _____.

W: _____ _____ _____ _____ it for a larger size?

What does the woman suggest the man do?

(A) Ask for a refund

(B) Purchase footwear

(C) Exchange an item

(D) Contact a shop clerk

2. CheckLink DL159 CD2-35

W: Excuse me, has this _____ for the computer _____ already?

M: No, it's still _____. We can _____ _____ free of charge.

What does the man offer the woman?

(A) Fast delivery

(B) Replacement of an item

(C) A full refund

(D) Free repair

PART 4 説明文問題

Practice!

音声を聞いて空所の語句を書き取り、設問に対する最も適切な選択肢を選びましょう。

1.　　　　　　　　　　　　　　　 **CheckLink**　　DL160　　CD2-36

If you are thinking about ＿＿＿＿＿＿ an online meeting from home, please use a ＿＿＿＿＿＿ . There are ＿＿＿＿＿＿ types with good functions, so I can ＿＿＿＿＿＿ ＿＿＿＿＿＿ ＿＿＿＿＿＿ a good one.

What does the speaker offer to do?

(A) Download software

(B) Purchase a drink

(C) Choose a device

(D) Meet the listener

2.　　　　　　　　　　　　　　　 **CheckLink**　　DL161　　CD2-37

Before you ＿＿＿＿＿＿ a jacket, shirt, trousers, or skirt, you can ＿＿＿＿＿＿ ＿＿＿＿＿＿ any of them in our store so that you can check ＿＿＿＿＿＿ ＿＿＿＿＿＿ ＿＿＿＿＿＿.

What does the speaker suggest the listeners do?

(A) Try on clothing

(B) Exchange items

(C) Use free shipping

(D) Complete an order form

PART 5 短文穴埋め問題

Practice!　　　CheckLink　　DL162～165　　CD2-38

空所に入る正しい語句を選んで書き、文を完成させましょう。その後で、正解の根拠となる部分に下線を引きましょう。

1. More than ten customers _____ new bicycles yesterday.

   (A) purchase　　(B) purchasing　　(C) purchased　　(D) will purchase

2. Pride Footwear _____ delivering items overseas next month.

   (A) starts　　(B) start　　(C) started　　(D) will start

3. Mr. Gomez _____ his computer with a new one, and it is functioning smoothly now.

   (A) replaced　　(B) will replace　　(C) replaces　　(D) replacing

4. If you _____ more than two items, you will receive a five percent discount.

   (A) orders　　(B) ordered　　(C) will order　　(D) order

PART 6 長文穴埋め問題

Practice!　　　CheckLink　　DL166～167　　CD2-39 ～ CD2-40

空所に入る正しい語句を選んで書き、文書を完成させましょう。その後で、正解の根拠となる部分に下線を引きましょう。

1. We guarantee your satisfaction with all of our products. Please try out _____ features at our store locations.

(A) its　　(B) his　　(C) their　　(D) your

2. CD Gallery features a famous photographer, Yuta Ono. _____ photos are available for purchase online.

(A) His　　(B) Their　　(C) Its　　(D) Our

PART 7 読解問題

Practice!   CheckLink   DL168   CD2-41

文書を読んで、設問に対する最も適切な選択肢を選びましょう。その後で、正解の根拠となる部分にそれぞれ下線を引きましょう。

Satoshi [11:36 A.M.]	Hi, Laura. We've just received another large order for coffee beans, so I'll send the order form to you by e-mail.
Laura [11:37 A.M.]	Thanks.
Satoshi [11:38 A.M.]	Do you know if we have enough?
Laura [11:38 A.M.]	Let me get back to you.
Laura [11:40 A.M.]	Some are currently out of stock, but we have enough for the order we just received.
Satoshi [11:42 A.M.]	Good. So now we can go on to the shipping process.

1. Why did Satoshi contact Laura?
   (A) To return some items
   (B) To share information
   (C) To give a full refund
   (D) To send a receipt

2. At 11:38 A.M., what does Laura mean when she writes, "Let me get back to you"?
   (A) She is waiting for an e-mail.
   (B) She will check with a customer.
   (C) She needs time to check the stock.
   (D) She has purchased the item before.

TOEIC
Mini Test

PART 1
CheckLink   DL169 ~ 170   CD2-42 ~ CD2-43

Select the one statement that best describes what you see in the picture.

1.

Ⓐ Ⓑ Ⓒ Ⓓ

2.

Ⓐ Ⓑ Ⓒ Ⓓ

PART 2
CheckLink   DL171 ~ 177   CD2-44 ~ CD2-50

Select the best response to the question or statement.

3. Mark your answer on your answer sheet.　　　　　　　　　Ⓐ Ⓑ Ⓒ

4. Mark your answer on your answer sheet.　　　　　　　　　Ⓐ Ⓑ Ⓒ

5. Mark your answer on your answer sheet.　　　　　　　　　Ⓐ Ⓑ Ⓒ

6. Mark your answer on your answer sheet.　　　　　　　　　Ⓐ Ⓑ Ⓒ

7. Mark your answer on your answer sheet.　　　　　　　　　Ⓐ Ⓑ Ⓒ

8. Mark your answer on your answer sheet.　　　　　　　　　Ⓐ Ⓑ Ⓒ

9. Mark your answer on your answer sheet.　　　　　　　　　Ⓐ Ⓑ Ⓒ

PART 3

CheckLink DL178 ~ 179 CD2-51 ~ CD2-52

Select the best response to each question.

10. Where are the speakers?

(A) At a grocery store

(B) At a photo studio

(C) At a museum

(D) At an appliance store

11. What does the man offer to do?

(A) Exchange items

(B) Download a valid coupon

(C) Give a product demonstration

(D) Correct a receipt

12. What does the man give the women?

(A) A brochure

(B) An order form

(C) A warranty

(D) A customer satisfaction survey

PART 4

CheckLink  DL180 ~ 181 CD2-53 ~ CD2-54

Select the best response to each question.

13. Where is the announcement being made?

(A) At a clothing store

(B) At a furniture store

(C) At a supermarket

(D) At a station

14. What does the speaker suggest the listeners do?

(A) Apply for membership

(B) Bring a bag

(C) Ask for assistance

(D) Write a review

15. Why do the listeners need to provide a receipt?

(A) To receive a coupon

(B) To return an item

(C) To get an order form

(D) To join a program

PART 5

Select the best answer to complete the sentence.

16. You ------- a refund after we have completed the process.
(A) will get
(B) got
(C) get
(D) have gotten

17. Mr. Goto ------- an order form to the Thomson Institute by e-mail yesterday.
(A) sends
(B) will send
(C) has sent
(D) sent

18. Ms. Louis ------- her shoes after she found the color did not match her dress.
(A) exchanges
(B) exchanged
(C) exchange
(D) will exchange

19. Starwide Florist ------- the varieties of flowers next month.
(A) will increase
(B) increased
(C) increase
(D) has increased

20. When Ms. Nakashima bought three boxes of water last week, she ------- an extra shipping fee for fast delivery.
(A) pays
(B) pay
(C) paid
(D) will pay

21. Our most popular jacket is out of stock now, and it ------- at the store by the end of the month.
(A) arrives
(B) arrived
(C) had arrived
(D) will arrive

22. If you ------- more than 50 dollars, your items will be delivered free of charge.
(A) spent
(B) spending
(C) spend
(D) spends

23. This coupon is not valid because it ------- on May 31.
(A) will expire
(B) expired
(C) expires
(D) expiring

PART 6

Select the best answer to complete the text.

Questions 24-27 refer to the following advertisement.

Great News for Crown Sports Members!

The summer sale starts on July 1 at all Crown Sports locations! Our members will be offered up to 40 percent off regular prices of our complete line of sporting

------- . It ranges from camping gear to baseball bats and balls to
  24.

swim wear to footwear. Why don't you get ready for all ------- summer events,
                             25.

both indoors and outdoors? For purchases of more than 100 dollars, you will get free shipping.

The sale ------- until the end of July. ------- .
      26.   **27.**

---

24. (A) events
(B) equipment
(C) season
(D) courses

25. (A) his
(B) their
(C) your
(D) its

26. (A) will last
(B) lasting
(C) lasted
(D) last

27. (A) We'll see you in August!
(B) We apologize for the delay.
(C) Keep the receipt until then.
(D) Don't wait too long!

Select the best answer for each question.

Questions 28-30 refer to the following online chat discussion.

Andy [9:11 A.M.]   Chelsea, I've checked the kitchen, and I'm afraid we don't have enough potatoes for today's reservations.

Chelsea [9:17 A.M.]   I'm leaving home in a few minutes. I can drop by Ann's Grocery and buy some. Do we need any other ingredients?

Andy [9:20 A.M.]   Thanks. Can you get five cartons of milk? There are various kinds, but please buy the red package with white lines. It is popular among our customers.

Chelsea [9:20 A.M.]   Sure, I will.

Andy [9:23 A.M.]   Take your time. I'll clean the tables for you today.

Chelsea [9:25 A.M.]   Great! Thanks.

---

28. What most likely is Andy's job?

(A) Cashier
(B) Truck driver
(C) Chef
(D) Salesperson

29. At 9:20 A.M., what does Chelsea mean when she writes, "Sure, I will"?

(A) She will leave home early.
(B) She will make a purchase.
(C) She will send a package.
(D) She will call customers.

30. What does Andy offer to do for Chelsea?

(A) Do some cleaning
(B) Buy some items
(C) Make a reservation
(D) Repair tables

TOEIC
Vocabularies & Phrases

Unit 6 Offices

次の Unit 6 に登場する TOEIC 頻出語句＆フレーズです。

| Step 1 | 意味を確認した上で、音声に続いて音読してみましょう。 |
| Step 2 | 再度音声を聞きながら、意味を思い出してみましょう。 |

🎧 DL192 ⚫CD2-58

□□□ arrangement	□□□ 名手配、準備
□□□ assignment	□□□ 名（割り当てられた）仕事
□□□ colleague	□□□ 名同僚
□□□ coworker	□□□ 名同僚
□□□ inspect	□□□ 動点検する
□□□ install	□□□ 動設置する
□□□ malfunction	□□□ 名故障　動故障する
□□□ matter	□□□ 名問題、事柄　動重要である
□□□ notice	□□□ 名掲示、通知　動気が付く
□□□ out of order	□□□ 故障して
□□□ overtime	□□□ 名残業　形時間外の　副時間外に
□□□ permit	□□□ 名許可（証）　動許可する
□□□ photocopier	□□□ 名コピー機
□□□ properly	□□□ 副正常に、適切に
□□□ relocation	□□□ 名移転
□□□ renovation	□□□ 名改修
□□□ responsibility	□□□ 名責任
□□□ supply	□□□ 名備品、供給　動供給する
□□□ temporary	□□□ 形一時的な、臨時の
□□□ urgent	□□□ 形緊急の

Unit 6 Offices

学習目標
- □ 「オフィス」に関する語句・表現を覚える
- □ 主語と動詞の一致を学ぶ

PART 1 写真描写問題

人物の位置・場所② 2人のパターン

2人の人物の位置関係では、お互いの位置関係や2人と物の位置関係がポイントです。

They're sitting **around** a table.（彼らはテーブルの周りに座っている）

across from ...（…の向かいに）、by ...（…のそばに）、on +「物」、in +「場所」など、人物の位置関係や場所が適切かどうかを確認しましょう。

Practice!　　CheckLink　　DL193　　CD2-59

音声を聞いて空所の語句を書き取り、写真を最も適切に表す選択肢を選びましょう。

(A) They're _____ _____ the _____.

(B) They're _____ _____ the _____.

(C) They're _____ _____ _____ each other.

(D) They're _____ _____ the _____.

PART 2 応答問題

WH疑問文⑥ How+ α で始まる疑問文

How+ α で「頻度」や「期間」などを尋ねることができます。How often（どのくらいの頻度）、How long（どのくらいの期間）、How many（どのくらいの数）、How much（どのくらいの量）など、How+ α を正確に聞き取らないと応答を選べません。

Practice!　　CheckLink　　DL194 ~ 195　　CD2-60　~　CD2-61

音声を聞いて空所の語句を書き取り、最も適切な応答の選択肢を選びましょう。

1. How _____ have you _____ here?

(A) I _____ _____ yesterday.

(B) _____ _____ _____.

(C) _____ my _____.

2. How _____ are the elevators _____?

(A) _____ _____ the _____.

(B) They don't _____ _____.

(C) _____ a _____.

PART 3 会話問題

会話の流れから話し手の発言の意図をくみ取る

話し手の意図に関する問題では、What does the man mean when he says, "You're right"?（男性は"You're right"という発言で、何を意味していますか）や、Why does the woman say, "That's not surprising"?（女性はなぜ"That's not surprising"と言っていますか）のように、発言の意図が問われます。基本的に前の流れを受けての発言となるため、会話の展開に対する理解が求められます。

Practice!

音声を聞いて空所の語句を書き取り、設問に対する最も適切な選択肢を選びましょう。

1. CheckLink DL196 CD2-62

W: Would you like to _____ a _____?

M: I'm fine. _____ already _____ the _____.

What does the man mean when he says, "I'm fine"?

(A) He feels good.

(B) He does not need to use a machine.

(C) He needs to finish an urgent matter.

(D) He agrees to work overtime.

2. CheckLink DL197 CD2-63

M: Did you _____ _____ for _____ software?

W: No. That's Ryan's assignment. Only he has a _____ to do it.

Why does the woman say, "That's Ryan's assignment"?

(A) To introduce a colleague

(B) To provide a reason

(C) To offer a temporary task

(D) To ask for a permit

直前のトークの展開から話し手の発言の意図をくみ取る

Part 4においても、What does the speaker mean when she says, "I'll get back to you later"? (話し手は "I'll get back to you later" という発言で、何を意味していますか) や、Why does the speaker say, "Make sure to check the notice"? (話し手はなぜ "Make sure to check the notice" と言っていますか) のように、発言の意図を問うものが出題されます。該当する発言の直前の話の展開を理解するようにしましょう。

Practice!

音声を聞いて空所の語句を書き取り、設問に対する最も適切な選択肢を選びましょう。

1. ♻CheckLink 🎧 DL198 ◉ CD2-64

This is to remind you that the _____ on the first floor is _____ _____ _____. The _____ will _____ _____ this afternoon. I'm sure it won't take long.

What does the speaker mean when she says, "I'm sure it won't take long"?

(A) A machine will be available soon.

(B) She has an urgent task.

(C) The listener needs to work overtime.

(D) Office supplies will be ready.

2. ♻CheckLink 🎧 DL199 ◉ CD2-65

As you know, our _____ _____ is _____ for March 1. We have only a week. Please check your _____ on the _____ board.

Why does the speaker say, "We have only a week"?

(A) To correct a mistake

(B) To inform listeners of the schedule change

(C) To suggest renewing a subscription

(D) To encourage listeners to act quickly

PART 5 短文穴埋め問題

主語と動詞の一致
例えば、主語が単数の場合、be動詞の現在形はis、過去形はwas、一般動詞の現在形にはsまたはesが付くように、主語に対応した動詞を使う必要があります。主語が複数であれば、be動詞の現在形はare、過去形はwere、一般動詞の現在形にはsまたはesが付きません。主語と動詞が離れている場合には特に注意しましょう。

Practice!　　　　 CheckLink 🎧 DL200 ~ 203 💿 CD2-66

空所に入る正しい語句を選んで書き、文を完成させましょう。その後で、正解の根拠となる部分に下線を引きましょう。

1. Responsibilities of the manager _____ assigning tasks to members, and giving permits to work overtime.

(A) include　　(B) includes　　(C) including　　(D) is included

2. Arrangements for temporary work space _____ completed yesterday.

(A) was　　(B) is　　(C) were　　(D) be

3. If one of the photocopiers _____, please contact the maintenance team.

(A) malfunction　　(B) malfunctioning　　(C) were malfunctioned　　(D) malfunctions

4. The elevators in the building _____, and now they are working properly.

(A) was inspected　　(B) will inspect　　(C) were inspected　　(D) has inspected

PART 6 長文穴埋め問題

代名詞③ まとめ
基本的にPart 6の代名詞を問う設問では、文脈を関連付けて読み取る力が測られています。前の文を参考に「誰」や「何」を特定しながら解答しましょう

Practice!　　　　 CheckLink 🎧 DL204 ~ 205 💿 CD2-67 ~ 💿 CD2-68

空所に入る正しい語句を選んで書き、文書を完成させましょう。その後で、正解の根拠となる部分に下線を引きましょう。

1. If you have an urgent matter, ask your coworkers for help. _____ contact information is listed in the attached document.

(A) His　　(B) Their　　(C) Your　　(D) Its

2. The supply room will be renovated next month. During that period, if you need to access _____, you will need a temporary security card.

(A) it　　(B) them　　(C) you　　(D) him

PART 7 読解問題

文挿入問題① キーワードや文自体の意味を手がかりにする

文を挿入する箇所を選ぶ設問では、挿入する文にあるキーワード（代名詞や話を展開させる表現など）や文自体の意味を手がかりにして、空所に入れた場合に前後関係として適切な展開となる箇所を特定しましょう。例えば、挿入する文にThisとあれば、その前の文にThisが指すものがありますし、挿入する文にHowever（しかし）とあれば、その前の文の内容を逆転させることがわかります。

Practice!

CheckLink　DL206　CD2-69

文書を読んで、設問に対する最も適切な選択肢を選びましょう。その後で、正解の根拠となる部分にそれぞれ下線を引きましょう。

From: Bart Saito, Property Manager
To: All employees

This is to remind you that renovation of exterior walls and floor tiles is scheduled for Friday, 7:00 P.M. You are required to leave the office by 6:00 P.M. The work will take three days. — [1] —. Also, before you leave the office on Friday, please clean your desk and do not leave anything on the floor. — [2] —. For further information, please look at the notice posted in the lobby. — [3] —. If you have any questions or concerns, please feel free to contact me at extension 221 or at b.saito@standandme.com. — [4] —.

---

1. What is the purpose of the notice?
   (A) To reschedule a project
   (B) To provide a permit
   (C) To give a reminder
   (D) To give contact information

2. In which of the positions marked [1], [2], [3], and [4] does the following sentence best belong?

   "Therefore, you are not allowed to enter the building over the weekend."
   (A) [1]
   (B) [2]
   (C) [3]
   (D) [4]

76

TOEIC
Mini Test

PART 1

Select the one statement that best describes what you see in the picture.

1.

Ⓐ Ⓑ Ⓒ Ⓓ

2.

Ⓐ Ⓑ Ⓒ Ⓓ

PART 2

Select the best response to the question or statement.

3. Mark your answer on your answer sheet.   Ⓐ Ⓑ Ⓒ

4. Mark your answer on your answer sheet.   Ⓐ Ⓑ Ⓒ

5. Mark your answer on your answer sheet.   Ⓐ Ⓑ Ⓒ

6. Mark your answer on your answer sheet.   Ⓐ Ⓑ Ⓒ

7. Mark your answer on your answer sheet.   Ⓐ Ⓑ Ⓒ

8. Mark your answer on your answer sheet.   Ⓐ Ⓑ Ⓒ

9. Mark your answer on your answer sheet.   Ⓐ Ⓑ Ⓒ

PART 3

Select the best response to each question.

10. What are the speakers discussing?
   (A) Inspecting a building
   (B) Ordering office supplies
   (C) Preparing for a presentation
   (D) Training some staff

11. What does the man mean when he says, "It's still new"?
   (A) The warranty covers the damage.
   (B) The product should not be out of order.
   (C) He has never used the equipment.
   (D) Information has been updated.

12. What will the man probably do next?
   (A) Call a repairperson
   (B) Visit a client
   (C) Set up equipment
   (D) Get some food

PART 4

Select the best response to each question.

13. What is the topic of the talk?
   (A) A company relocation
   (B) An upcoming renovation
   (C) An equipment malfunction
   (D) A new work assignment

14. What does the speaker mean when she says, "I don't think I need to tell you this"?
   (A) The listeners already know the process.
   (B) The listeners understand their job responsibilities.
   (C) The listeners are not allowed to work overtime.
   (D) The listeners got information from their coworkers.

15. What does the speaker ask about?
   (A) A work detail
   (B) A request for time off
   (C) A topic to discuss
   (D) A parking permit

PART 5

Select the best answer to complete the sentence.

16. Job responsibilities for each worker
------- on the wall.
(A) posted
(B) is posted
(C) to post
(D) are posted

17. Temporary workers at KS
Corporation ------- to get a permit for
overtime.
(A) needing
(B) need
(C) needs
(D) is needed

18. A parking permit for employees
------- their name, department, and
the expiration date.
(A) contain
(B) containing
(C) contains
(D) to contain

19. A good arrangement of desks -------
communication among employees.
(A) increasing
(B) increase
(C) to increase
(D) increases

20. Work assignments for next month
------- in the attached file.
(A) are included
(B) to include
(C) includes
(D) is included

21. Five employees at the factory -------
the evening shift.
(A) working
(B) works
(C) work
(D) to work

22. Design software with various
functions ------- on this computer.
(A) are installed
(B) installing
(C) is installed
(D) have been installed

23. Information on all of Synstars'
products ------- in the company
brochure.
(A) is provided
(B) will provide
(C) are provided
(D) have provided

Select the best answer to complete the text.

Questions 24-27 refer to the following e-mail.

To: All employees
From: Factory manager
Date: February 13
Subject: Regular inspection

All employees,

This is to inform you that the regular factory inspection has been -------. Some
24.
areas were pointed out for improvement. Most importantly, equipment such as
hard hats and gloves must be put in the right place after use. -------.
25.
By the way, some of the machines were out of order. Therefore, we have decided
to replace -------. If any machines don't work properly in the future, please -------
26.   **27.**
me know.

---

24. (A) completed
(B) delayed
(C) cancelled
(D) arranged

26. (A) it
(B) us
(C) you
(D) them

25. (A) Thank you for working overtime.
(B) Other points are listed in the
attached file.
(C) When it has been installed, you
will be informed.
(D) You are required to have a permit
to do so.

27. (A) ask
(B) tell
(C) let
(D) inspect

PART 7

CheckLink DL229 CD2-85

Select the best answer for each question.

Questions 28-30 refer to the following e-mail.

To:	Design team
From:	Glenn Richardson
Date:	December 15
Subject:	Software

Hi,

This is to remind you that the new design software must be installed by the end of the week. — [1] —. The software is very different from the one we are now using, so we will have a training session from 2:00 P.M. to 3:30 P.M. on December 21. Jeff Mines is an expert on the software. — [2] —.

I would like everyone to join the session. — [3] —. If you have any urgent matter, you can talk to Jeff personally to arrange some time, or ask your colleagues to show you how to use the software. If you have any questions or concerns, don't hesitate to contact me. — [4] —.

Glenn

28. What is the purpose of the e-mail?
(A) To change some work assignments
(B) To allow staff to work overtime
(C) To announce an urgent problem
(D) To ask members to attend a session

29. Who would contact Jeff Mines?
(A) A person who has not installed new software
(B) A person who has questions
(C) A person who cannot attend the session
(D) A person who has joined the team recently

30. In which of the positions marked [1], [2], [3], and [4] does the following sentence best belong?

"You can learn a lot from him."
(A) [1]
(B) [2]
(C) [3]
(D) [4]

TOEIC
Vocabularies & Phrases

Unit 7 **Clients**

次の Unit 7 に登場する TOEIC 頻出語句＆フレーズです。

Step 1 意味を確認した上で、音声に続いて音読してみましょう。
Step 2 再度音声を聞きながら、意味を思い出してみましょう。

DL230　CD3-02

□□□ agreement	□□□	名合意
□□□ apologize	□□□	動謝罪する
□□□ approve	□□□	動承認する
□□□ consider	□□□	動検討する、考慮する
□□□ construction	□□□	名建設
□□□ contract	□□□	名契約
□□□ deadline	□□□	名締め切り、期限
□□□ decision	□□□	名決定
□□□ due	□□□	形…の期限の
□□□ handle	□□□	動対処する、取り扱う
□□□ in charge of	□□□	…を担当している
□□□ inquiry	□□□	名問い合わせ
□□□ manufacturer	□□□	名製造業者、メーカー
□□□ negotiate	□□□	動交渉する
□□□ progress	□□□	名進展、発展、前進
□□□ quantity	□□□	名量
□□□ renew	□□□	動更新する
□□□ respond	□□□	動対応する、応答する
□□□ solution	□□□	名解決（策）
□□□ solve	□□□	動解決する

Unit 7 Clients

学習目標
- ☐ 「顧客」に関する語句・表現を覚える
- ☐ 能動態・受動態を学ぶ

PART 1 写真描写問題

人物の位置・場所③ 3人以上のパターン

3人以上の人物の位置関係は、以下のように全員に共通すること、または明らかに異なる1人のことが描写されます。

They're talking **in front of** a monitor.（彼らはモニターの前で話している）

One of the women is standing **behind** a desk.（女性の1人は机の後ろに立っている）

Practice!

CheckLink DL231 CD3-03

音声を聞いて空所の語句を書き取り、写真を最も適切に表す選択肢を選びましょう。

(A) They're _____ the _____.

(B) One of the men is _____ _____ _____ the _____.

(C) They're _____ _____ the _____.

(D) One of the women is _____ _____ _____ the _____.

PART 2 応答問題

Yes/No疑問文① Yes/Noで答えるパターン

Yes/No疑問文は、"Do you ...?"や"Are you ...?"などだけでなく、その後を聞き取れないと内容を理解できません。また、応答についてもYes/Noだけで判断せずに、その後に続く内容が質問の応答になっていることを理解できるリスニング力が求められます。

Practice!

CheckLink DL232～233 CD3-04 ～ CD3-05

音声を聞いて空所の語句を書き取り、最も適切な応答の選択肢を選びましょう。

1. _____ you _____ _____ Mr. Mori?

(A) I _____ the _____.

(B) _____, I _____ _____.

(C) _____, I _____ have it.

2. Did the _____ _____ the _____?

(A) _____, it's _____.

(B) About _____ .

(C) _____ , he _____ it.

PART 3 会話問題

Practice!

音声を聞いて空所の語句を書き取り、設問に対する最も適切な選択肢を選びましょう。

1. CheckLink DL234 CD3-06

M: Do you _____ _____
   to _____ the _____
   this week?
W: I'm _____ _____
   _____ before my _____
   _____.

Monday	Factory visit
Tuesday	Dentist
Wednesday	Team meeting
Thursday	Business trip to Boston

Look at the graphic. When will the speakers probably have a negotiation?

(A) On Monday
(B) On Tuesday
(C) On Wednesday
(D) On Thursday

2. CheckLink DL235 CD3-07

W: Did Ms. Park _____ a _____ on
   the _____ ?
M: She wanted to go for _____, but she
   _____ only _____
   _____ _____ a month.

Bronze	$500/month
Silver	$900/month
Gold	$1200/month
Platinum	$1800/month

Look at the graphic. Which plan will Ms. Park probably choose?

(A) Bronze
(B) Silver
(C) Gold
(D) Platinum

PART 4 説明文問題

図表問題① 選択肢に並んでいない情報を特定する

Part 3と同様に、トークの内容と図表の内容を関連付けて解答します。図表には2種類の情報があり、そのうち1種類が選択肢に並んでいます。選択肢に並んでいないほうの情報をトークから特定し、その情報に対応する選択肢を選びましょう。

Practice!

音声を聞いて空所の語句を書き取り、設問に対する最も適切な選択肢を選びましょう。

1.

CheckLink   DL236   CD3-08

We're _____ _____ the quantity of our order. We'd like to order 10 more T-shirts. We _____ for the _____.

Quantity	Item
15	Bags
25	Flags
30	T-shirts
100	Brochures

Look at the graphic. Which quantity needs to be changed?

(A) 15

(B) 25

(C) 30

(D) 100

2.

CheckLink   DL237   CD3-09

Now we've been working hard to _____ the _____. As I'm _____ _____ _____ the _____ project, I'd like to show you around the building. Could you come to the _____ on the day the _____ _____ begins?

May 10	Phase 1
May 17	Phase 2
May 24	Phase 3
May 31	Phase 4

Look at the graphic. What day are the listeners asked to be available?

(A) May 10

(B) May 17

(C) May 24

(D) May 31

PART 5 短文穴埋め問題

能動態・受動態

能動態とは主語が動作を行う際に使われる動詞の形で、We solved the problem. (私たちは問題を解決した) のように使われます。一方で、受動態とは主語が動作を受ける際に使われる形で、The problem was solved. (問題は解決された) のように使われます。「主語と動詞」や「動詞と目的語」の関係を読み取って、能動態か受動態かを判断しましょう。

Practice!

ⓒ CheckLink　🎧 DL238～241　💿 CD3-10

空所に入る正しい語句を選んで書き、文を完成させましょう。その後で、正解の根拠となる部分に下線を引きましょう。

1. The manager _____ the plan to sign the contract.

   (A) approved　(B) approving　(C) was approved　(D) to approve

2. The problem should _____ by the end of the week.

   (A) handle　(B) be handled　(C) handling　(D) be handling

3. Our service representatives _____ inquiries from customers within two business days.

   (A) be answered　(B) to answer　(C) answering　(D) answer

4. The contract must _____ before the expiration date.

   (A) renew　(B) renewing　(C) be renewed　(D) has renewed

PART 6 長文穴埋め問題

時制① 前後の文の内容から判断する

Part 6の時制問題ではwill solveとsolvedのように異なる時制の選択肢が並んでいます。空所のある文を読むだけでは解けないものがほとんどなので、前後の文の内容から空所に入る動詞が過去か未来かなどを判断しましょう。

Practice!

ⓒ CheckLink　🎧 DL242～243　💿 CD3-11　～　💿 CD3-12

空所に入る正しい語句を選んで書き、文書を完成させましょう。その後で、正解の根拠となる部分に下線を引きましょう。

---

1. The payment is due next Friday. We _____ it by the due date.

(A) pay　(B) will pay　(C) paid　(D) have paid

---

2. We _____ with PDX Manufacturing. They offered a discount, and we agreed to sign the contract.

(A) will negotiate　(B) negotiating　(C) negotiate　(D) negotiated

複数の文書に関する問題① 2つの情報を組み合わせる

複数の文書に関する問題では、それぞれの文書に散らばる情報を関連付けて解答することが求められます。設問で求められている情報が1カ所で見つからない場合、2つの文書の情報を組み合わせて解答しましょう。

Practice!　CheckLink　DL244　CD3-13

文書を読んで、設問に対する最も適切な選択肢を選びましょう。その後で、正解の根拠となる部分にそれぞれ下線を引きましょう。

Work Schedule (Phase 4)			
October 3-4	Wiring & Installing lights	**October 8-10**	Planting trees
October 5-7	Interior work	**October 11-13**	Painting walls

To: Michelle Cohen
From: Gregg Simon
Subject: Work schedule

Dear Ms. Cohen,

We have almost completed Phase 3, but because of the recent rain, we weren't able to make progress as scheduled. We apologize for the delay, but the schedule for Phase 4 needs to be changed. Work in the building will be the same, but planting trees and painting walls need to be pushed back by one day.

Gregg Simon

---

1. What kind of business does Mr. Simon most likely work for?
   (A) A catering company
   (B) A travel agency
   (C) A real estate agency
   (D) A construction company

2. When will planting trees probably be completed?
   (A) On October 8
   (B) On October 9
   (C) On October 10
   (D) On October 11

PART 1

↻CheckLink 🎧 DL245 ~ 246   ~

Select the one statement that best describes what you see in the picture.

1.

ⒶⒷⒸⒹ

2.

ⒶⒷⒸⒹ

PART 2

↻CheckLink 🎧 DL247 ~ 253   ~ ● CD3-22

Select the best response to the question or statement.

3. Mark your answer on your answer sheet.   ⒶⒷⒸ

4. Mark your answer on your answer sheet.   ⒶⒷⒸ

5. Mark your answer on your answer sheet.   ⒶⒷⒸ

6. Mark your answer on your answer sheet.   ⒶⒷⒸ

7. Mark your answer on your answer sheet.   ⒶⒷⒸ

8. Mark your answer on your answer sheet.   ⒶⒷⒸ

9. Mark your answer on your answer sheet.   ⒶⒷⒸ

PART 3

Select the best response to each question.

Price List	
Carpet	$200.00
Windows	$170.00
Furniture	$230.00
Computers	$140.00

11. Look at the graphic. Which price will be discounted?
(A) $200.00
(B) $170.00
(C) $230.00
(D) $140.00

10. Where does the woman probably work?
(A) A rental service
(B) A cleaning company
(C) A department store
(D) A real estate agency

12. What will the man do next?
(A) Respond to an e-mail
(B) Negotiate with another company
(C) Sign the contract
(D) Handle some problems

PART 4

Select the best response to each question.

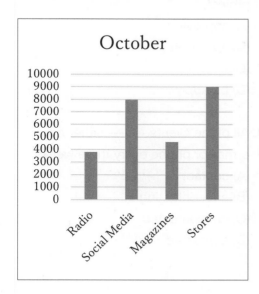

14. Look at the graphic. What was the biggest increase in October?
(A) Radio
(B) Social Media
(C) Magazines
(D) Stores

15. What will the listeners probably do next?
(A) Watch a video
(B) Discuss a solution
(C) Ask questions
(D) Fill out a form

13. What is the problem?
(A) A system did not work properly.
(B) A project has not made progress.
(C) A price was wrong.
(D) A shipment was late.

Select the best answer to complete the sentence.

16. Payment for the construction
   supplies must ------- by the due
   date.
   (A) make
   (B) makes
   (C) be made
   (D) made

17. Please ------- to customer inquiries
   within 24 hours.
   (A) be responded
   (B) response
   (C) responded
   (D) respond

18. The plan about the construction
   project ------- to the client last week.
   (A) provides
   (B) providing
   (C) was provided
   (D) to provide

19. Mr. Trevor ------- a mechanical
   problem with his team.
   (A) handled
   (B) was handled
   (C) handling
   (D) to be handled

20. Discounts will not ------- after
   December 1.
   (A) be considering
   (B) be considered
   (C) consider
   (D) considering

21. The systems engineers ------- the
   deadline by working overtime.
   (A) met
   (B) meets
   (C) be met
   (D) meeting

22. The plan needs to ------- by the
   manufacturer before starting the
   project.
   (A) approving
   (B) approval
   (C) approve
   (D) be approved

23. All of the clients ------- either by
   e-mail or phone every three weeks.
   (A) contact
   (B) are contacting
   (C) are contacted
   (D) contacted

PART 6

Select the best answer to complete the text.

Questions 24-27 refer to the following e-mail.

To: Mana Greene
From: Katsumi Ikeyama
Date: June 6
Subject: Contract

Dear Ms. Greene,

Thank you for offering a trial period. As a construction company, we are happy with the quality of your building materials. Therefore, we ------- the contract with
                                                                                                    24.
you. The management will ------- it later today.
                              25.

We would like to start using your blocks as soon as possible at our current
construction sites. -------. We look forward to working with ------- for years to
                      26.   **27.**
come.

Best regards,

Katsumi Ikeyama

---

24. (A) signed
(B) signing
(C) will sign
(D) had signed

25. (A) replace
(B) renew
(C) solve
(D) approve

26. (A) I will send the order soon.
(B) It has been completed.
(C) We work with a car manufacturer.
(D) We apologize for the delay.

27. (A) them
(B) you
(C) it
(D) some

PART 7

Select the best answer for each question.

Questions 28-30 refer to the following advertisement and form.

McKinley Repair Service

Need to solve car problems? You can visit us or our experienced mechanics will repair your car at your home or office. Just schedule an appointment with our app. If you are a long-time customer and have a customer code, please put it in the customer code box. If you don't have one, just leave it blank. If you need to use our service before 9:00 A.M. or after 10:00 P.M., there will be an additional $10 fee.

(APPLY)

Name: [Josh Steiner]
Address: [810 Grayson Street]
Customer Code: [91021]
Service: [X] Oil change [ ] Tire change [ ] Repair [ ] Painting
          [ ] Other [   ]

Request

Any day is fine with me this week, but I would like you to come to my place at 7:15 A.M. because I usually leave before 8:00 A.M.

---

28. What is the purpose of the advertisement?
(A) To provide customer reviews
(B) To suggest an appointment
(C) To announce a business relocation
(D) To introduce a new service

29. Who most likely is Mr. Steiner?
(A) A new resident at Grayson Street
(B) A worker at McKinley Repair Service.
(C) A long-time customer of McKinley Repair Service
(D) An app designer

30. What will Mr. Steiner probably do?
(A) Visit McKinley Repair Service
(B) Reserve a room
(C) Purchase tires
(D) Pay an additional fee

TOEIC
Vocabularies & Phrases

Unit 8 Recruiting

次のUnit 8に登場するTOEIC頻出語句＆フレーズです。

| Step 1 | 意味を確認した上で、音声に続いて音読してみましょう。 |
| Step 2 | 再度音声を聞きながら、意味を思い出してみましょう。 |

⬇ DL268 💿 CD3-30

☐☐☐ applicant	☐☐☐ 名応募者、志願者
☐☐☐ application	☐☐☐ 名応募（書類）
☐☐☐ apply for	☐☐☐ …に応募する
☐☐☐ attach	☐☐☐ 動添付する、くっつける
☐☐☐ candidate	☐☐☐ 名候補者
☐☐☐ career	☐☐☐ 名経歴、職業
☐☐☐ degree	☐☐☐ 名学位、（温度・角度などの）度
☐☐☐ evaluate	☐☐☐ 動評価する
☐☐☐ experience	☐☐☐ 名経験　動経験する
☐☐☐ fill out	☐☐☐ 記入する
☐☐☐ interview	☐☐☐ 名面接　動面接する
☐☐☐ job opening	☐☐☐ 仕事の空き、求人
☐☐☐ opportunity	☐☐☐ 名機会
☐☐☐ qualification	☐☐☐ 名資格
☐☐☐ qualified	☐☐☐ 形資格のある、適任の
☐☐☐ reference	☐☐☐ 名照会先、身元保証
☐☐☐ reliable	☐☐☐ 形信頼できる
☐☐☐ require	☐☐☐ 動求める、必要とする
☐☐☐ résumé	☐☐☐ 名履歴書
☐☐☐ submit	☐☐☐ 動提出する

Recruiting

学習目標
□ 「採用・求人」に関する語句・表現を覚える
□ 動名詞・不定詞を学ぶ

PART 1 写真描写問題

光景② 現在進行形が使われるパターン

「物」が主語の場合でも、現在進行形が使われる場合があります。

A letter **is lying** on the desk.（手紙が机の上に置かれている）

lying（置かれてある）や hanging（掛かっている）など主語となる物の状態、on the wall（壁に）や from the ceiling（天井から）など他の物との位置関係の聞き取りがポイントとなります。

Practice! CheckLink DL269 CD3-31

音声を聞いて空所の語句を書き取り、写真を最も適切に表す選択肢を選びましょう。

(A) Some chairs are _____ a desk.

(B) A board is _____ a _____.

(C) A screen is _____ on the _____.

(D) A shelf is _____ a _____.

PART 2 応答問題

Yes/No疑問文② Yes/Noで答えないパターン

Yes/No疑問文に対する応答でも、Yes/Noで始まるものが正解とは限りません。Yes/Noを省略して質問者が求める情報をすぐに伝えたり、Yes/Noの代わりに別の肯定・否定を表す表現が使われたりします。

Practice! CheckLink DL270〜271 CD3-32 〜 CD3-33

音声を聞いて空所の語句を書き取り、最も適切な応答の選択肢を選びましょう。

1. Is _____ _____ _____ for the position?

   (A) I _____ it's _____.

   (B) No, he didn't get the _____.

   (C) That's a _____ _____.

2. Have you _____ the _____ _____ yet?

   (A) Yes, I'd like to _____ _____ it.

   (B) I'm _____ I didn't have _____.

   (C) I think I'm _____.

PART 3 会話問題

会話から話し手の職業を判断する
会話に出てくる男性や女性の職業や職場について問われることがよくあります。会話文を聞きながら、話し手がどんな職業についているのか、どのような職場で働いているのかを判断できるようにしましょう。

Practice!

音声を聞いて空所の語句を書き取り、設問に対する最も適切な選択肢を選びましょう。

1. CheckLink DL272 CD3-34

W: _____to Bridge Hyper _____. How can I _____ you today?

M: Hi, my name is Henry Jones. I'm _____to _____ for the _____ position.

Who most likely is the man?

(A) A librarian

(B) A salesperson

(C) A fitness instructor

(D) A mechanic

2. CheckLink DL273 CD3-35

M: Hi, Betty. Who do you think is the most _____ for our _____ position?

W: Well. I think Ms. Newman has a lot of _____ and is the _____ _____ for our _____.

Who most likely are the speakers?

(A) Hotel clerks

(B) Store managers

(C) Travel agents

(D) Journalists

PART 4 説明文問題

トークから話し手・聞き手の職業を判断する

Part 3と同様、職業や働いている場所について問われることがよくあります。ただし、Part 4では話し手だけでなく、聞き手についても問われる可能性があります。話し手、聞き手がどのような人物なのかを意識しながらトークを聞きましょう。

Practice!

音声を聞いて空所の語句を書き取り、設問に対する最も適切な選択肢を選びましょう。

1.   CheckLink   DL274   CD3-36

As we _____ at the _____, you're _____ to _____ two _____ from your _____ employers.

Who most likely is the speaker?

(A) A shop owner

(B) A job recruiter

(C) A marketing consultant

(D) An architect

2.   CheckLink   DL275   CD3-37

Hello, Mr. Coleman. _____ is Caroline Gibson from Pitman _____.
We _____ your _____ for our _____ _____ position.

Who most likely is the listener?

(A) A receptionist

(B) A fashion designer

(C) A photographer

(D) A software engineer

PART 5 短文穴埋め問題

動名詞・不定詞

動名詞（動詞のing形）と不定詞（to＋動詞の原形）は文の中で名詞の働きができます。動詞の目的語として使われる場合、動名詞・不定詞のどちらか一方しか取らない動詞があります。また、前置詞の後ろで使われる場合は動名詞のみを使うことができます。

Practice! ⟲ CheckLink 🎧 DL276 ~ 279 🔘 CD3-38

空所に入る正しい語句を選んで書き、文を完成させましょう。その後で、正解の根拠となる部分に下線を引きましょう。

1. Mr. Hunter is considering _____ for a new job.
   (A) apply   (B) to apply   (C) applying   (D) applied

2. Walters Supermarket decided _____ some part-time workers.
   (A) to hire   (B) hire   (C) hired   (D) hiring

3. Every applicant hopes _____ from the hiring office soon.
   (A) to hearing   (B) hears   (C) hearing   (D) to hear

4. Before _____ the document, be sure to update your contact information.
   (A) attach   (B) attaching   (C) to attach   (D) attached

PART 6 長文穴埋め問題

時制② 適切な時制を選ぶ

Part 6の時制問題では、空所のある文だけを見ても答えが求められないことが多くあります。前後の文の内容をヒントに、空所に入る適切な時制を選びましょう。

Practice! ⟲ CheckLink 🎧 DL280 ~ 281 🔘 CD3-39 ~ 🔘 CD3-40

空所に入る正しい語句を選んで書き、文書を完成させましょう。その後で、正解の根拠となる部分に下線を引きましょう。

1. Gibson Food Services _____ the first round of interviews. All the applicants showed that they had suitable qualifications for the job.

(A) conducts   (B) will conduct   (C) conducted   (D) to conduct

2. I just asked Ms. Wilson to give us references by the end of next week. We _____ all the people to see her performances at previous jobs.

(A) will contact   (B) contact   (C) contacted   (D) are contacted

概要に関する問題② 文書全体に共通して述べられていることを見つけ出す

概要に関する問題では、What is the purpose of ...?のように目的が問われたり、What is described in ...?、What is ... mainly about?のように文書の内容について問われたりします。これらの設問に解答するには、文書全体にわたって共通して述べられていることを見つけ出す力が求められます。1問目に出題されることが多いですが、他の設問に解答して内容を把握した後に解くと、早く解答できる場合があります。

Practice!

文書を読んで、設問に対する最も適切な選択肢を選びましょう。その後で、正解の根拠となる部分にそれぞれ下線を引きましょう。

Job Opening: Project Manager at Progressive Solutions

> **Main responsibilities:**
> • Create marketing plans
> • Conduct marketing campaigns
> • Supervise project members

The successful candidate should have excellent management skills such as supervising team members, assigning proper tasks, and finishing projects in time. He or she should also have a degree in marketing-related areas.

Any interested candidates should apply by e-mail along with a cover letter, résumé, and a letter of recommendation to Robert Johnson at **rjohnson@psolutions.com**.

---

1. What is the purpose of the Web page?

(A) To promote a product

(B) To find a marketing specialist

(C) To introduce an employee

(D) To get customer feedback

2. What is NOT mentioned as a responsibility of the project manager?

(A) Performing sales campaigns

(B) Managing a team

(C) Making ideas for marketing

(D) Hiring a project member

TOEIC
Mini Test

PART 1

CheckLink   DL283 ~ 284   CD3-42 ~ CD3-43

Select the one statement that best describes what you see in the picture.

1.

Ⓐ Ⓑ Ⓒ Ⓓ

2.

Ⓐ Ⓑ Ⓒ Ⓓ

PART 2

CheckLink   DL285 ~ 291   CD3-44 ~ CD3-50

Select the best response to the question or statement.

3. Mark your answer on your answer sheet.   Ⓐ Ⓑ Ⓒ

4. Mark your answer on your answer sheet.   Ⓐ Ⓑ Ⓒ

5. Mark your answer on your answer sheet.   Ⓐ Ⓑ Ⓒ

6. Mark your answer on your answer sheet.   Ⓐ Ⓑ Ⓒ

7. Mark your answer on your answer sheet.   Ⓐ Ⓑ Ⓒ

8. Mark your answer on your answer sheet.   Ⓐ Ⓑ Ⓒ

9. Mark your answer on your answer sheet.   Ⓐ Ⓑ Ⓒ

PART 3

CheckLink   DL292 ~ 293    CD3-51 ~ CD3-52

Select the best response to each question.

10. Who most likely are the speakers?
- (A) Employees of a manufacturing company
- (B) Customers of a car dealer
- (C) Editors of a publishing company
- (D) Salespeople of a furniture store

11. What did the man do last week?
- (A) He conducted an interview.
- (B) He hired a sales manager.
- (C) He made a marketing plan.
- (D) He attended a workshop.

12. What will the woman probably do next?
- (A) Talk to a manager
- (B) Prepare for a meeting
- (C) Fill out a form
- (D) Contact a candidate

PART 4

CheckLink   DL294 ~ 295   CD3-53 ~ CD3-54

Select the best response to each question.

13. Where does the speaker work?
- (A) At a box office
- (B) At a restaurant
- (C) At an electronics store
- (D) At a department store

14. Who most likely is the listener?
- (A) A career coach
- (B) A job applicant
- (C) A store owner
- (D) An event planner

15. What is the listener asked to do?
- (A) Confirm a schedule
- (B) Purchase an item
- (C) Visit an office
- (D) Provide some information

Select the best answer to complete the sentence.

16. Ms. Brown finished ------- all the applications submitted by yesterday.
(A) reviewing
(B) to review
(C) reviewed
(D) reviews

17. Companies expect ------- reliable and qualified applicants at a job fair.
(A) meet
(B) meeting
(C) to meet
(D) met

18. Mr. Smith is interested in ------- a master's degree in business.
(A) get
(B) getting
(C) gets
(D) to get

19. Ms. Donovan declined to ------- the job offer from the East Marine Hotel.
(A) accept
(B) accepts
(C) accepting
(D) accepted

20. The interviewers avoided ------- too many interviews within a day.
(A) have
(B) had
(C) to have
(D) having

21. Owen Web Design Inc. has decided ------- an opportunity for its employees to learn business skills.
(A) to providing
(B) provide
(C) to provide
(D) providing

22. Mr. Ford is looking forward to ------- a career support seminar at school.
(A) attend
(B) attending
(C) attends
(D) attended

23. Hack Engineering postponed ------- a final decision about the number of new hires.
(A) to make
(B) make
(C) to be made
(D) making

Select the best answer to complete the text.

Questions 24-27 refer to the following e-mail.

From: Sandy Collins
To: Peter Jackson
Subject: Application
Date: June 8

Dear Mr. Jackson,

My name is Sandy Collins. I ------- your advertisement on PlanningJobs.com.
24.
Today, I am writing to apply for the architect position. I am currently working for TMK Works in Denver as an assistant designer. -------, we are moving to Los
25.
Angeles for personal reasons in August. -------. I would like to grow my designing
26.
skills with your experienced staff.

I am attaching my résumé to this e-mail. If you have any questions, please feel free to contact me.

I hope ------- back from you soon.
27.

Sincerely,
Sandy Collins

---

24. (A) see
(B) will see
(C) saw
(D) seeing

25. (A) However
(B) For example
(C) Therefore
(D) Instead

26. (A) The advertisement was posted on a weekly basis.
(B) This design was highly evaluated.
(C) You are responsible for customer services.
(D) Your company is well-known for designing various buildings.

27. (A) hears
(B) to hear
(C) heard
(D) hearing

Select the best answer for each question.

Questions 28-30 refer to the following e-mail.

From:	James Chen
To:	Ronald Williams
Subject:	Assistant chef position
Date:	September 20

Dear Mr. Williams,

My name is James Chen. I am writing to apply for the position of assistant chef listed on Richie's Steak House's Web site. I have been working at a small restaurant for two years, helping chefs make various dishes. I know your restaurant requires three years of experience. I am wondering if I have a chance to be considered as a candidate. I have strong communication skills and am ready to work nights and weekends. Attached is my résumé. If you need some other documents, I can submit them immediately.

I look forward to hearing from you.

Sincerely,

James Chen

28. What is the e-mail mainly about?
(A) An opening of a restaurant
(B) An inquiry about a job
(C) A new steak dish
(D) Hours of operation

29. Who most likely is Mr. Williams?
(A) A restaurant customer
(B) A Web designer
(C) A restaurant employee
(D) A meat supplier

30. According to the e-mail, what can Mr. Chen do for Mr. Williams?
(A) Evaluate a restaurant
(B) Make a new menu
(C) Fill out an online form
(D) Give additional information

TOEIC
Vocabularies & Phrases

Unit 9 **Personnel**

次のUnit 9に登場するTOEIC頻出語句＆フレーズです。

Step 1　意味を確認した上で、音声に続いて音読してみましょう。
Step 2　再度音声を聞きながら、意味を思い出してみましょう。

🎧 DL306　💿 CD3-58

□□□ board of directors	□□□ 取締役会
□□□ branch	□□□ 图支社、支店
□□□ department	□□□ 图部（門）、部署
□□□ division	□□□ 图部（門）、部署
□□□ efficient	□□□ 形効率のよい、有能な
□□□ evaluation	□□□ 图評価、査定
□□□ executive	□□□ 图重役　形重役の
□□□ farewell	□□□ 图別れ、送別会
□□□ headquarters	□□□ 图本社、本部
□□□ human resources	□□□ 人事（部）、人材
□□□ management	□□□ 图経営（者）
□□□ orientation	□□□ 图オリエンテーション、説明会
□□□ participant	□□□ 图参加者
□□□ payroll	□□□ 图給与
□□□ personnel	□□□ 图人事（部）、社員
□□□ promotion	□□□ 图昇進、販売促進
□□□ resign	□□□ 動辞任する
□□□ retire	□□□ 動退職する、退く
□□□ transfer	□□□ 图転勤、移動
	動転勤する、転勤させる
□□□ vice president	□□□ 副社長

Personnel

PART 1 写真描写問題

人物の動作④ 身に着けているものに関する表現パターン

人物の写真では身に着けているものについても述べられます。

She's **wearing a hat.** (彼女は帽子をかぶっている)

glassesやhandbagなどに対し、wear (身に着けている) やput on (着る、身に着ける)、take off (脱ぐ、外す) など適切な状態や動作を選びます。

Practice!　　CheckLink 🎧 DL307 💿 CD3-59

音声を聞いて空所の語句を書き取り、写真を最も適切に表す選択肢を選びましょう。

(A) He's _____ on _____.

(B) He's _____ a _____.

(C) He's _____ _____.

(D) He's _____ his _____.

PART 2 応答問題

Yes/No疑問文③ 間接疑問文

When will the meeting start?のようなWH疑問文がDo you know when the meeting will start?のように別の文に組み込まれているものを間接疑問文といいます。Yes/No疑問文のようですが、WH疑問文に対する応答が正解になる場合があります。

Practice!　　CheckLink 🎧 DL308 ~ 309 💿 CD3-60 ~ 💿 CD3-61

音声を聞いて空所の語句を書き取り、最も適切な応答の選択肢を選びましょう。

1. Do you _____ _____ the
new employee _____ will be held?

(A) No, the _____ _____
will _____.

(B) In the _____ room.

(C) At the _____ of the month.

2. I don't _____ _____
_____ office Brian was
_____ to.

(A) I think he's in _____ now.

(B) No, the _____ department.

(C) Near _____ _____.

PART 3 会話問題

会話から話し手たちの間で起きている問題を把握する
Part 3 の会話では、話し手たちの間で起きている問題や、その解決策について話しているみ、どんな問題が起き、話し手たちはどのようにそれらに対処しているかに注目しましょう。

Practice!

音声を聞いて空所の語句を書き取り、設問に対する最も適切な選択肢を選びましょう。

1. CheckLink DL310 CD3-62

W: I need to _____ out some documents for the workshop but the _____ is _____ again.

M: I see. I think you can use _____ in the _____ _____.

What is the problem?
(A) The photocopier is running out of paper.
(B) The printer does not work properly.
(C) Some documents include mistakes.
(D) The workshop is delayed.

2. CheckLink DL311 CD3-63

M: Hi, Rachel. I just read your e-mail, but I _____ the _____ of the performance _____ was _____.

W: Really? Oh, that's right. I'll e-mail everyone the _____ version _____.

What problem does the man mention?
(A) An e-mail has not been received.
(B) A service is no longer available.
(C) A performance was canceled.
(D) Some information is incorrect.

PART 4 説明文問題

トークから話し手が報告している問題を把握する

Part 4では話し手が電話のメッセージなどで問題を報告していることがよくあります。「時間に遅れる」「商品が足りない」「機械が壊れている」など、問題と思われる部分を聞き逃さないようにしましょう。

Practice!

音声を聞いて空所の語句を書き取り、設問に対する最も適切な選択肢を選びましょう。

1. CheckLink DL312 CD3-64

I just _____ that we haven't _____ anyone who'll give
a _____ at Mr. Fox's _____ _____. That was
_____ yesterday.

What is the problem?

(A) A farewell party was not held.

(B) An item is missing from the list.

(C) Preparations are behind schedule.

(D) An executive is unable to attend the event.

2. CheckLink DL313 CD3-65

Hi, Donald. I finished _____ my team members and tried to _____
on to the _____ _____. But there's _____ _____
with it.

What problem does the speaker report?

(A) A system is unavailable.

(B) A product is out of stock.

(C) A member has not arrived.

(D) A meeting is too long.

PART 5 短文穴埋め問題

比較

複数のものを比較するために比較級や最上級が使われます。比較級は形容詞や副詞の終わりにerを付けるか、前にmoreを置きます。最上級は形容詞や副詞の終わりにestを付けるか、前にmostを置きます。また、単語によっては不規則変化するものもあります。

Practice!

CheckLink　DL314～317　CD3-66

空所に入る正しい語句を選んで書き、文を完成させましょう。その後で、正解の根拠となる部分に下線を引きましょう。

1. This year's payroll cost is a little ＿＿＿＿＿＿＿＿ than that of last year.
   (A) high　(B) highly　(C) higher　(D) highest

2. Ms. Charlton is the ＿＿＿＿＿＿＿＿ of all the workers in the overseas division.
   (A) efficient　(B) most efficient　(C) efficiently　(D) more efficient

3. The downtown area is the ＿＿＿＿＿＿＿ location for a corporate headquarters in the city.
   (A) good　(B) well　(C) better　(D) best

4. Mr. Maxwell will resign as vice president ＿＿＿＿＿＿＿ than expected.
   (A) earliest　(B) earliness　(C) early　(D) earlier

PART 6 長文穴埋め問題

時制③ まとめ

選択肢に現在、過去、未来など異なる時制の動詞が並んでいる場合は、前後の文の時制や日付などの時に関する表現をヒントにして、適切な時制を選びましょう。

Practice!

CheckLink　DL318～319　CD3-67　～　CD3-68

空所に入る正しい語句を選んで書き、文を完成させましょう。その後で、正解の根拠となる部分に下線を引きましょう。

1. This year's new employee orientation ＿＿＿＿＿＿＿＿ at our headquarters on April 4. We have received positive feedback from the participants.

   (A) was held　(B) is held　(C) will be held　(D) has held

2. The Sydney branch of Fletcher Bank is scheduled to open at the end of September. Mr. Kent ＿＿＿＿＿＿＿＿ there to manage the branch.

   (A) is transferred　(B) was transferred　(C) transfers　(D) will be transferred

詳細な情報に関する問題② 問われている箇所を文書から探し出す

概要を問う設問では、文書全体を読まなければ答えがわからない場合がありますが、詳細な情報を問う設問では、文書の中で設問に関連する部分を読めば解答することができます。「どのような人が (who)」「どこで (where)」「いつ (when)」「何を (what)」「何のために (why)」「どのような方法で (how)」行うかについて問われます。設問で問われている部分を文書から素早く探し出し、言い換え表現に注意しながら答えを見つけましょう。

Practice!   ↻CheckLink 🎧 DL320 ◉ CD3-69

文書を読んで、設問に対する最も適切な選択肢を選びましょう。その後で、正解の根拠となる部分にそれぞれ下線を引きましょう。

From: Sharon Green

To: Team managers

Subject: Yearly Performance Evaluations

Date: November 20

Dear Managers,

We are going to start the yearly performance evaluations from December 1. You will be required to evaluate all your team members fairly. The deadline to submit all evaluations will be December 15. Your team members will also be required to submit a self-evaluation by December 10. Please remind them of this information.

Best Regards,

Sharon Green, Head of Human Resources

---

1. By when should managers submit performance evaluations?

  (A) November 20

  (B) December 1

  (C) December 10

  (D) December 15

2. What are managers asked to do?

  (A) Tell their members about the deadline

  (B) Submit a self-evaluation

  (C) Hold a team meeting

  (D) Visit the human resources office

TOEIC
Mini Test

PART 1

CheckLink DL321 ~ 322 CD3-70 ~ CD3-71

Select the one statement that best describes what you see in the picture.

1.

Ⓐ Ⓑ Ⓒ Ⓓ

2.

Ⓐ Ⓑ Ⓒ Ⓓ

PART 2

CheckLink DL323 ~ 329 CD3-72 ~ CD3-78

Select the best response to the question or statement.

3. Mark your answer on your answer sheet.   Ⓐ Ⓑ Ⓒ

4. Mark your answer on your answer sheet.   Ⓐ Ⓑ Ⓒ

5. Mark your answer on your answer sheet.   Ⓐ Ⓑ Ⓒ

6. Mark your answer on your answer sheet.   Ⓐ Ⓑ Ⓒ

7. Mark your answer on your answer sheet.   Ⓐ Ⓑ Ⓒ

8. Mark your answer on your answer sheet.   Ⓐ Ⓑ Ⓒ

9. Mark your answer on your answer sheet.   Ⓐ Ⓑ Ⓒ

PART 3

  DL330 ~ 331 CD3-79 ~ CD3-80

Select the best response to each question.

10. What are the speakers discussing?
  (A) An instructor
  (B) A meeting agenda
  (C) A food delivery
  (D) A training session

11. What problem does the woman mention?
  (A) The schedule is already full.
  (B) The room is not big enough.
  (C) The projector does not work properly.
  (D) A meeting space has not been reserved.

12. What will the man probably do next?
  (A) Check room availability
  (B) E-mail participants
  (C) Visit the head office
  (D) Prepare some food

PART 4

CheckLink DL332 ~ 333 CD3-81 ~ CD3-82

Select the best response to each question.

13. What problem does the speaker mention?
  (A) The payroll will be low.
  (B) An employee is unavailable.
  (C) A computer is not working.
  (D) A form has not been received.

14. Who most likely is Ms. Newton?
  (A) A division manager
  (B) A new employee
  (C) A salesperson
  (D) A bank employee

15. What will Ms. Newton most likely do this week?
  (A) Open a bank account
  (B) Attend an orientation meeting
  (C) Finish a monthly report
  (D) Visit the personnel department

PART 5

Select the best answer to complete the sentence.

16. The new payroll system has been working ------- than the old one.
(A) well
(B) best
(C) good
(D) better

17. Developing human resources is the ------- thing in the management of a company.
(A) important
(B) most important
(C) more important
(D) importantly

18. This year's new employees are taking the orientation ------- than last year's.
(A) seriously
(B) most seriously
(C) more seriously
(D) serious

19. Mr. Potter is the employee who has changed departments the ------- in Spenser Food services.
(A) most
(B) much
(C) many
(D) more

20. Managers are asked to submit their evaluation reports no ------- than March 2.
(A) late
(B) later
(C) latest
(D) lately

21. The board of directors is ------- in training employees than hiring skilled people.
(A) interested
(B) interesting
(C) more interested
(D) most interested

22. Hudson Tech's executives are expecting the ------- sales performance in its twenty-year history.
(A) bad
(B) worse
(C) badly
(D) worst

23. The employees at Cowper Industries will be evaluated ------- than before.
(A) more frequently
(B) frequent
(C) most frequently
(D) frequently

PART 6

Select the best answer to complete the text.

Questions 24-27 refer to the following e-mail.

To: All Employees
From: Human Resources
Date: January 29
Subject: Mr. Lee's Retirement

Dear All:

As you may probably know, Mr. Jason Lee, vice president in Finance, is going to retire next month. He has been a ------- and loyal employee for over 30 years.
                                                      24.

-------. To express our appreciation, we ------- a farewell party on Friday,
  25.   **26.**

February 4 at the Center Hotel Ballroom. We are also planning ------- him a gift
                                                                 27.

there. If you have any questions, please contact Sheldon White in HR at swhite@pmsolutions.com.

---

24. (A) reliability
    (B) reliably
    (C) reliable
    (D) rely

25. (A) His strong leadership has contributed a lot to us.
    (B) We had the event at our head office.
    (C) Some employees resigned last month.
    (D) It is sometimes difficult to get a promotion.

26. (A) hold
    (B) will hold
    (C) held
    (D) holding

27. (A) giving
    (B) give
    (C) given
    (D) to give

Select the best answer for each question.

Questions 28-30 refer to the following e-mail.

To:	Sales Staff
From:	Connie Greystone
Subject:	Personnel Transfer
Date:	March 12

Dear Sales Staff,

I would like to announce that I am going to transfer from Philadelphia to our head office in New York next month. I wanted to stay and work with you longer, but I was offered a promotion and decided to accept it. This might be challenging for me, but I will try my best.

The new sales manager will be Fred Swanson. He is now working at the Boston branch and used to work at the Detroit branch, too. I've known him for a long time and I think you will quickly come to love him. I will introduce him to you when he visits us next week.

Sincerely,

Connie Greystone, Sales Manager

28. What is the purpose of the e-mail?
(A) To introduce a new employee
(B) To invite sales staff to a farewell party
(C) To announce a personnel change
(D) To confirm an appointment

29. Where does Ms. Greystone work?
(A) In Philadelphia
(B) In New York
(C) In Boston
(D) In Detroit

30. What will happen next week?
(A) Ms. Greystone will be transferred.
(B) The headquarters will be moved.
(C) New promotional campaigns will start.
(D) Mr. Swanson will meet sales staff.

TOEIC
Vocabularies & Phrases

Unit 10 Advertising

次のUnit 10に登場するTOEIC頻出語句＆フレーズです。

| Step 1 | 意味を確認した上で、音声に続いて音読してみましょう。 |
| Step 2 | 再度音声を聞きながら、意味を思い出してみましょう。 |

🎧 DL344　💿 CD4-02

□□□ advertise	□□□ 動宣伝する
□□□ attract	□□□ 動引きつける
□□□ brochure	□□□ 名パンフレット
□□□ campaign	□□□ 名キャンペーン
□□□ commercial	□□□ 名コマーシャル　形商業的な
□□□ consumer	□□□ 名消費者
□□□ coupon	□□□ 名クーポン
□□□ display	□□□ 名陳列　動陳列する
□□□ effective	□□□ 形効果的な
□□□ feedback	□□□ 名意見、反応
□□□ flyer	□□□ 名チラシ
□□□ free of charge	□□□ 無料で
□□□ impress	□□□ 動印象づける
□□□ last	□□□ 動続く
□□□ merchandise	□□□ 名商品
□□□ offer	□□□ 名申し出、提案　動提供する
□□□ satisfy	□□□ 動満足させる
□□□ selection	□□□ 名品ぞろえ、選択
□□□ specialize in	□□□ 専門とする
□□□ voucher	□□□ 名割引券

Unit 10 Advertising

学習目標
- ☐ 「広告・宣伝」に関する語句・表現を覚える
- ☐ 前置詞を学ぶ

PART 1 写真描写問題

光景③ 位置関係の表現パターン

「物」と「物」の位置関係は前置詞（句）を使って表されます。

A magazine is **under** the table.（雑誌がテーブルの下にある）

in front of（前に）や behind（後ろに）などの位置関係を表す前置詞（句）や、side by side（並んで）や in a row（一列に並んで）などの定型表現も覚えましょう。

Practice!　　ⒸCheckLink　🎧DL345　💿CD4-03

音声を聞いて空所の語句を書き取り、写真を最も適切に表す選択肢を選びましょう。

(A) Books are _____ in a _____.

(B) A pen is _____ _____
　　　a _____.

(C) A cup is _____ a _____.

(D) _____ are _____ a newspaper.

PART 2 応答問題

付加疑問文

This coupon is valid, isn't it?（このクーポンは有効ですよね？）のように、文の後ろに短い疑問文が付いているものを付加疑問文といいます。「…ですよね？」と相手に内容を確認する際に用いられます。応答の仕方は Yes/No 疑問文と同じです。

Practice!　　ⒸCheckLink　🎧DL346 ~ 347　💿CD4-04 ~ 💿CD4-05

音声を聞いて空所の語句を書き取り、最も適切な応答の選択肢を選びましょう。

1. This _____ is _____
of _____, _____ it?
(A) I think it was very _____.
(B) Yes, you can _____ it.
(C) The _____ _____ will
start soon.

2. We haven't _____ _____
from _____, _____ we?
(A) No, we'll _____ it next week.
(B) We have a _____ _____
of products.
(C) They _____ in marketing.

3人の会話の中で2人の共通点を見つける
Part 3の会話は男女3人の間で行われることもあります。What will the men probably do next?などのように、男性2人または女性2人に共通する意見や行動、職場が問われます。2人に共通するものが何かを見つけましょう。

Practice!

音声を聞いて空所の語句を書き取り、設問に対する最も適切な選択肢を選びましょう。

1.　　　　　　　　　　　　　　　　　　　　　　　CheckLink　　DL348　　CD4-06

W: Does _____ have any _____ for the new _____?

M1: _____ don't we ask Sandy to _____ it?

M2: I think so, too. She has a lot of _____.

What do the men suggest?
(A) Including a voucher in a flyer
(B) Having a wide selection of merchandise
(C) Asking someone for assistance
(D) Giving a product free of charge

2.　　　　　　　　　　　　　　　　　　　　　　　CheckLink　　DL349　　CD4-07

M: Have you _____ _____ you should do for the opening _____?

W1: Not yet. We'll probably _____ 20% _____ on all our products.

W2: We're also _____ giving a gift.

What are the women doing?
(A) Planning an opening campaign
(B) Displaying some products
(C) Printing out a special coupon
(D) Meeting some consumers

> **トークの目的を理解する**
> Part 4では1人の話し手が何かの目的のために話をしています。「仕事の依頼」「人物の紹介」「予定の変更」「情報の提供」など、話し手が何の目的で話をしているのか、冒頭部分に特に注意をして聞きましょう。

Practice!

音声を聞いて空所の語句を書き取り、設問に対する最も適切な選択肢を選びましょう。

1.　　　　　　　　　　　　　　　　　　CheckLink　🎧 DL350　◎ CD4-08

_____ customers. We're _____ to _____ that we're having a _____ sale at our _____ _____ on the second floor.

What is the purpose of the talk?

(A) To advertise a new shop
(B) To provide a discount voucher
(C) To respond to an inquiry
(D) To attract more customers

2.　　　　　　　　　　　　　　　　　　CheckLink　🎧 DL351　◎ CD4-09

Thank you for coming to this meeting. Today I have an _____ to _____ about the _____ _____ . It'll _____ _____ the end of the month.

What is the purpose of the meeting?

(A) To share some information
(B) To explain a consumer trend
(C) To introduce staff members
(D) To discuss a TV commercial

PART 5 短文穴埋め問題

前置詞

前置詞には期間や目的を表すforや、手段や期限を表すby、時や場所を表すat、in、onなどがあります。それぞれの前置詞のイメージを理解し、文脈に合う前置詞を選びましょう。また、一緒によく使われる動詞や形容詞とセットで覚えましょう。

Practice!

CheckLink   DL352 ~ 355   CD4-10

空所に入る正しい語句を選んで書き、文を完成させましょう。その後で、正解の根拠となる部分に下線を引きましょう。

1. All the rooms in this building are used _____ commercial purposes.
   (A) at   (B) for   (C) about   (D) from

2. Customers are satisfied _____ a selection of quality merchandise.
   (A) into   (B) between   (C) to   (D) with

3. Desmond Advertising Agency specializes _____ social media marketing.
   (A) on   (B) in   (C) as   (D) by

4. We are expecting to get feedback from consumers _____ ten days.
   (A) within   (B) since   (C) among   (D) of

PART 6 長文穴埋め問題

接続表現① 前後の文の内容を理解する

文と文の間の接続表現が問われる問題では、「セール→**therefore**（それゆえ）/**as a result**（その結果）→売上増」「広告費削減→**however**（しかし）/**fortunately**（幸運にも）→売上増」など、前後の文の内容を理解し、話の流れに合う適切な表現を選びましょう。

Practice!

CheckLink   DL356 ~ 357   CD4-11 ~ CD4-12

空所に入る正しい語句を選んで書き、文書を完成させましょう。その後で、正解の根拠となる部分に下線を引きましょう。

1. The flyer with some discount vouchers attracted a lot of shoppers to the store. _____, sales did not increase as much as we expected.

(A) Therefore   (B) Finally   (C) Fortunately   (D) However

2. The newspaper advertisement was not so effective. _____, we will try an online advertisement for our new product.

(A) Also   (B) Therefore   (C) However   (D) For example

PART 7 読解問題

推測させる問題② 言い換えを意識する

What is suggested about ...? (…について何がわかりますか) のような答えを推測させる設問では、本文に書かれてある表現とは別の表現が設問や選択肢に書かれてあります。例えば、What is suggested about the store?という設問に対し、本文にはOur store is 5 minutes from the station.と書かれ、正解の選択肢にはIt is easily accessible.のように書かれます。言い換えられていることを常に意識して問題を解きましょう。

Practice!

 CheckLink　DL358　CD4-13

文書を読んで、設問に対する最も適切な選択肢を選びましょう。その後で、正解の根拠となる部分にそれぞれ下線を引きましょう。

Fast Web TV Free Trial!

Register today for Fast Web TV and receive a one-month free trial of our service. Our service provides a wide selection of programs including news, sports, music, and entertainment. We are sure you will be impressed with our service.

If you are satisfied after the trial period, you can join our basic membership for $4.95 a month. For more information about the different membership levels, check out our Web site at www.fastwebtv.com.

---

1. What is being advertised?
   (A) TV commercials
   (B) Online programs
   (C) Movie tickets
   (D) Internet banking

2. What is suggested about the fees?
   (A) They are more expensive than other companies.
   (B) There are some price options.
   (C) A yearly payment is available.
   (D) They include Internet access.

TOEIC
Mini Test

PART 1

CheckLink DL359 ~ 360 CD4-14 ~ CD4-15

Select the one statement that best describes what you see in the picture.

1.

Ⓐ Ⓑ Ⓒ Ⓓ

2.

Ⓐ Ⓑ Ⓒ Ⓓ

PART 2

CheckLink DL361 ~ 367 CD4-16 ~ CD4-22

Select the best response to the question or statement.

3. Mark your answer on your answer sheet.   Ⓐ Ⓑ Ⓒ

4. Mark your answer on your answer sheet.   Ⓐ Ⓑ Ⓒ

5. Mark your answer on your answer sheet.   Ⓐ Ⓑ Ⓒ

6. Mark your answer on your answer sheet.   Ⓐ Ⓑ Ⓒ

7. Mark your answer on your answer sheet.   Ⓐ Ⓑ Ⓒ

8. Mark your answer on your answer sheet.   Ⓐ Ⓑ Ⓒ

9. Mark your answer on your answer sheet.   Ⓐ Ⓑ Ⓒ

PART 3

CheckLink · DL368 ~ 369 · CD4-23 ~ CD4-24

Select the best response to each question.

10. What type of business do the speakers probably work at?
(A) A fitness center
(B) A music school
(C) A restaurant
(D) A cooking school

11. What do the men suggest?
(A) Advertising on TV
(B) Sending a greeting card
(C) Making a flyer
(D) Offering a discount

12. What will the woman do next?
(A) Bring some brochures
(B) Write a newspaper article
(C) Make a phone call
(D) Visit a company office

PART 4

CheckLink · DL370 ~ 371 · CD4-25 ~ CD4-26

Select the best response to each question.

13. What is the purpose of the talk?
(A) To offer a selection of items
(B) To announce a campaign
(C) To describe a store layout
(D) To explain a return policy

14. What should the listeners do to receive a cup?
(A) Visit the store's Web site
(B) Present a coupon
(C) Provide some feedback
(D) Go to a service counter

15. What are the listeners asked to do?
(A) Bring their friends to the store
(B) Visit the store more frequently
(C) Select from different options
(D) Watch a TV commercial

Select the best answer to complete the sentence.

16. Victor Appliances usually sends brochures to customers ------- e-mail.
(A) to
(B) into
(C) by
(D) with

17. New houses for sale were advertised ------- local newspapers yesterday.
(A) in
(B) at
(C) under
(D) for

18. A new line of consumer electronics is ------- display in the store window.
(A) within
(B) on
(C) of
(D) in

19. Refreshments will be provided to participants free ------- charge at the opening event.
(A) around
(B) to
(C) of
(D) as

20. Customers were impressed ------- beautiful flyers made by professional designers.
(A) to
(B) about
(C) with
(D) from

21. The coupon for a free dessert is valid ------- the end of the month.
(A) behind
(B) by
(C) on
(D) until

22. Morgan Motors has been running a TV commercial ------- the last five years.
(A) over
(B) since
(C) from
(D) at

23. Shoppers at Ames Mall are asked to choose one ------- two complimentary gifts.
(A) into
(B) between
(C) under
(D) among

PART 6

Select the best answer to complete the text.

Questions 24-27 refer to the following advertisement.

XTZ Cleaning Services

Do you need to clean your work space? ------- is better than XTZ Cleaning
                                              24.

Services. We ------- in corporate customers and have the highest standards of
             25.

professional cleaning. Our workers are trained in using the latest cleaning

technology. No cleaning job is too difficult for us. -------, we have a long list of
                                                26.

satisfied customers. Our service is available 24 hours a day, seven days a week.

-------. Don't hesitate to call us at 555-8008. You can also visit our Web site at
  27.

www.xtzcleaning.com. We look forward to hearing from you!

---

24. (A) Nobody
    (B) Anybody
    (C) Somebody
    (D) Everybody

25. (A) specialized
    (B) will specialize
    (C) specialize
    (D) are specialized

26. (A) However
    (B) As a result
    (C) For example
    (D) Instead

27. (A) This is the most effective tool to
          clean.
    (B) We were impressed by your work
          space.
    (C) Cleaning jobs are sometimes
          difficult.
    (D) We can clean your office during
          the night.

PART 7

Select the best answer for each question.

Questions 28-30 refer to the following advertisement.

 Return & Recycle Shop

Return & Recycle Shop will have its special clearance sale from August 24-30. All merchandise in the shop marked clearance will be on sale for 30-50 percent off the regular prices. The discount will be applied to the price at the register.

You can also sell your used goods for a higher rate than other shops. We will pay an additional 10 percent to customers who sell any used goods during the sale period.

Please note that any item will be carefully tested by our staff to check if it works properly. To receive the extra 10 percent, all items must meet our quality standards. If you have any questions, please feel free to ask our staff.

28. What is indicated about the sale?
  (A) It is held every month.
  (B) A discount coupon will be provided.
  (C) Some items are free of charge.
  (D) It will last for a week.

29. What is suggested about the shop?
  (A) It buys used items from customers.
  (B) It has several locations.
  (C) It is a family-owned business.
  (D) It was established ten years ago.

30. Why do store clerks check items?
  (A) To find out the brand name
  (B) To see if they are in good condition
  (C) To contact the manufacturer
  (D) To make a detailed report

TOEIC
Vocabularies & Phrases

Unit 11　**Media**

次のUnit 11に登場するTOEIC頻出語句＆フレーズです。

| Step 1 | 意味を確認した上で、音声に続いて音読してみましょう。 |
| Step 2 | 再度音声を聞きながら、意味を思い出してみましょう。 |

🎧 DL382　⊙ CD4-30

☐☐☐ according to	☐☐☐ …によれば、…に従って
☐☐☐ article	☐☐☐ 名記事
☐☐☐ author	☐☐☐ 名著者
☐☐☐ broadcast	☐☐☐ 名放送　動放送する
☐☐☐ copy	☐☐☐ 名部（数）
☐☐☐ critic	☐☐☐ 名批評家
☐☐☐ editor	☐☐☐ 名編集者
☐☐☐ feature	☐☐☐ 名特集記事　動呼び物にする、特集する
☐☐☐ forecast	☐☐☐ 名予測　動予測する
☐☐☐ issue	☐☐☐ 名号、問題
☐☐☐ journal	☐☐☐ 名雑誌、新聞
☐☐☐ latest	☐☐☐ 形最新の
☐☐☐ local	☐☐☐ 形地元の
☐☐☐ press conference	☐☐☐ 記者会見
☐☐☐ publish	☐☐☐ 動出版する
☐☐☐ quarterly	☐☐☐ 名季刊誌　形年４回の　副年４回
☐☐☐ submission	☐☐☐ 名提出、投稿
☐☐☐ subscribe	☐☐☐ 動定期購読する
☐☐☐ traffic jam	☐☐☐ 交通渋滞
☐☐☐ update	☐☐☐ 名最新情報　動更新する

Unit 11 Media

学習目標
- ☐ 「メディア」に関する語句・表現を覚える
- ☐ 接続詞を学ぶ

PART 1 写真描写問題

人物の動作⑤ 抽象的な言い換えパターン

人物の動作を表す文では、抽象的な表現も使われます。

He's holding some **reading material**. (彼は読み物を手に持っている)

例えば、男性が雑誌を手に持っている写真では、magazine（雑誌）という具体的な表現も使われますが、reading material（読み物）という抽象的な表現も使われるので注意しましょう。

Practice!　　CheckLink　DL 383　CD4-31

音声を聞いて空所の語句を書き取り、写真を最も適切に表す選択肢を選びましょう。

(A) He's playing a _____

_____.

(B) He's _____ some _____.

(C) He's _____ a piece of

_____.

(D) He's _____ by some

_____.

PART 2 応答問題

否定疑問文

Do you know him?の先頭の部分を否定の形にしたDon't you know him?（彼を知らないのですか）のような疑問文を否定疑問文といいます。普通の疑問文でも否定疑問文でも、応答は彼を知っていればYes, I do.、知らなければNo, I don't.となります。

Practice!　　CheckLink　DL384~385　CD4-32 ~ CD4-33

音声を聞いて空所の語句を書き取り、最も適切な応答の選択肢を選びましょう。

1. Don't you _____ to _____ _____ this _____?

   (A) No, that's a _____ _____.

   (B) She's not an _____ of it.

   (C) It's published _____.

2. Isn't the _____ _____ _____ to _____?

   (A) Yes, he's a _____ _____.

   (B) There's a _____ in the lobby.

   (C) Oh, I haven't _____ it yet.

127

PART 3 会話問題

会話内の特定の情報をキャッチする

「参加するイベント」「購入予定の商品」「スケジュールの変更点」など、会話の中で話し手たちが話す特定の情報が問われることがあります。問題文が流れる前に設問を先読みし、問われる点を理解しておくと、それらの情報を聞き逃しにくくなります。

Practice!

音声を聞いて空所の語句を書き取り、設問に対する最も適切な選択肢を選びましょう。

1.   CheckLink   DL 386   CD4-34

W: Hello, Mr. Hardy. Thanks for _____ me today. _____ the _____ design you requested.

M: That's great. I think this _____ the _____ of the new _____.

What does the woman show the man?

(A) A copy of a magazine

(B) A magazine cover

(C) A latest journal

(D) An author's profile

2.   CheckLink   DL 387   CD4-35

M: A lot of _____ are expected to come to the _____ _____. I don't think Meeting Room A is _____ enough.

W: OK. Can you make the _____ _____?

According to the man, what needs to be changed?

(A) The number of participants

(B) A meeting schedule

(C) A delivery of some food

(D) The location of an event

PART 4 説明文問題

トーク内の特定の情報をキャッチする

トークの中ではさまざまな話が展開されます。「製品やサービスのよい点・悪い点」「ウェブサイトで実施できる機能」「提出が求められる情報」など、問われる点を事前に理解し、聞き逃しのないようにしましょう。

Practice!

音声を聞いて空所の語句を書き取り、設問に対する最も適切な選択肢を選びましょう。

1.　　　　　　　　　　　　　　　　CheckLink 　DL 388 　CD4-36

Good evening. You're _____ to WYAT's _____ news. Today's _____ story is tomorrow's grand _____ of the _____ _____ in the city center.

What will open in the city center?

(A) A city library

(B) A furniture shop

(C) A car factory

(D) A shopping center

2.　　　　　　　　　　　　　　　　CheckLink 　DL 389 　CD4-37

This is Ted Lee with the _____ report. This morning it was _____, but in the afternoon it's _____ to be _____. _____ tuned for more _____.

What does Mr. Lee say about the weather this afternoon?

(A) The temperature will continue to rise.

(B) It is supposed to be fine.

(C) There will be a lot of clouds.

(D) It is the same as the last forecast.

PART 5 短文穴埋め問題

接続詞

接続詞が問われる問題では、接続詞が結ぶ2つの文の意味を考えて適切なものを選びます。接続詞には以下のようなものがあります。

if（もし…ならば）、unless（…でない限り）、when（…するとき）、while（…する間）、since（…以来、…だから）、because（…だから）、although（…だけれども）

Practice! CheckLink DL390～393 CD4-38

空所に入る正しい語句を選んで書き、文を完成させましょう。その後で、正解の根拠となる部分に下線を引きましょう。

1. _____ the weather is bad, the book signing event will be canceled.
   (A) So   (B) If   (C) Although   (D) Unless

2. We were late for a press conference _____ there was a traffic jam.
   (A) although   (B) until   (C) because   (D) but

3. Ms. Watson has subscribed to the quarterly journal _____ she became an editor.
   (A) since   (B) when   (C) or   (D) if

4. _____ Kemp's café was featured in a magazine, some information was wrong.
   (A) Since   (B) Unless   (C) And   (D) Although

PART 6 長文穴埋め問題

接続表現② 話の流れに合う表現を選ぶ

接続表現が問われる問題では、「大雨→in addition/moreover（さらに）→暴風」「急げ→otherwise（さもなければ）→遅刻」「階段→alternatively（代わりに）→エレベーター」など、話の流れに合う表現を選びましょう。

Practice! CheckLink DL394～395 CD4-39 ～ CD4-40

空所に入る正しい語句を選んで書き、文書を完成させましょう。その後で、正解の根拠となる部分に下線を引きましょう。

---

1. We must receive feedback from critics about the latest movies immediately. _____, we cannot include it in our next broadcast.

(A) Therefore   (B) Otherwise   (C) Alternatively   (D) Moreover

---

2. The event of the newly published magazine will offer a complimentary copy of the first issue. _____, a discount coupon for the next issue will be provided.

(A) For example   (B) However   (C) Otherwise   (D) In addition

PART 7 読解問題

Practice!　　　　　ⒸCheckLink　⬇ DL 396　◉ CD4-41

文書を読んで、設問に対する最も適切な選択肢を選びましょう。その後で、正解の根拠となる部分にそれぞれ下線を引きましょう。

New Sports Center to Open Next Month

October 12—In today's press conference, the city of Toronto announced that it will open a new sports center on November 1. On the first day, the mayor will deliver a speech to celebrate the opening.

The sports center features two large indoor gyms for basketball, volleyball, and other activities. In addition, other indoor facilities include a swimming pool, a training room, and a children's playroom.

The center is conveniently located near the city hall. The residents of the city can use the facilities for three dollars at a time.

---

1. The word "deliver" in paragraph 1, line 2, is closest in meaning to
  (A) carry
  (B) achieve
  (C) give
  (D) update

2. What is indicated about the center?
  (A) It is in the city office.
  (B) It is free for local residents.
  (C) It includes a facility for kids.
  (D) It hired professional instructors.

TOEIC
Mini Test

Select the one statement that best describes what you see in the picture.

1.

2.

Ⓐ Ⓑ Ⓒ Ⓓ   Ⓐ Ⓑ Ⓒ Ⓓ

Select the best response to the question or statement.

3. Mark your answer on your answer sheet.   Ⓐ Ⓑ Ⓒ

4. Mark your answer on your answer sheet.   Ⓐ Ⓑ Ⓒ

5. Mark your answer on your answer sheet.   Ⓐ Ⓑ Ⓒ

6. Mark your answer on your answer sheet.   Ⓐ Ⓑ Ⓒ

7. Mark your answer on your answer sheet.   Ⓐ Ⓑ Ⓒ

8. Mark your answer on your answer sheet.   Ⓐ Ⓑ Ⓒ

9. Mark your answer on your answer sheet.   Ⓐ Ⓑ Ⓒ

PART 3

Select the best response to each question.

10. Where does the man most likely work?
(A) At a restaurant
(B) At a supermarket
(C) At a hotel
(D) At a publishing company

11. What is missing from the article?
(A) A store address
(B) A link to a Web site
(C) Local news
(D) A submission schedule

12. What will the woman most likely do next?
(A) Subscribe to a magazine
(B) Call one of the critics
(C) Go to a store
(D) Contact her colleague

PART 4

Select the best response to each question.

13. Who most likely is Randy Matthews?
(A) A travel agent
(B) A tour guide
(C) A radio host
(D) A city official

14. What does the speaker say is causing the delay?
(A) A vehicle malfunction
(B) Weather conditions
(C) A public event
(D) Road construction

15. What will listeners hear next?
(A) An afternoon schedule
(B) Traffic rules
(C) A product demonstration
(D) Local information

Select the best answer to complete the sentence.

16. The TV station is planning to interview Ms. Hyde ------- she is the author of a bestselling book.
    (A) because
    (B) after
    (C) unless
    (D) although

17. ------- the quarterly magazine becomes popular, more people will subscribe to it.
    (A) But
    (B) If
    (C) Although
    (D) Unless

18. A technical issue occurred ------- a sports announcer was reporting live.
    (A) while
    (B) because
    (C) so
    (D) since

19. A business trend will be featured in both the September ------- October issues of the journal.
    (A) or
    (B) as
    (C) and
    (D) when

20. The news program begins at 7 P.M. just ------- the weather forecast finishes.
    (A) until
    (B) after
    (C) although
    (D) while

21. Readers can send their submissions either by filling out an online form ------- by e-mail.
    (A) and
    (B) before
    (C) when
    (D) or

22. Mr. Sharrock became a famous radio host ------- he had no experience in that field.
    (A) since
    (B) so
    (C) although
    (D) until

23. ------- we get permission from the city, we cannot start shooting a video outside.
    (A) So
    (B) If
    (C) Since
    (D) Unless

PART 6

Select the best answer to complete the text.

Questions 24-27 refer to the following article.

Chicago (February 13)—The Easton Business Journal for industry executives

------- on March 1. This journal provides tips about how to handle difficult issues
24.

in business. In every issue, business ------- are invited to share their experiences.
25.

-------. For example, it will share problem-solving skills or tips on how to manage
26.

people from different cultures. People can subscribe to a printed version of the

journal. -------, they can choose the online version.
27.

---

24. (A) will publish
   (B) has published
   (C) will be published
   (D) publishing

25. (A) professionals
   (B) broadcasts
   (C) submissions
   (D) meetings

26. (A) We need at least three years'
      experience.
   (B) It is quarterly according to the
      editor.
   (C) Readers will learn useful
      techniques.
   (D) Some local businesses were
      supported.

27. (A) Therefore
   (B) Alternatively
   (C) Personally
   (D) However

PART 7

Select the best answer for each question.

Questions 28-30 refer to the following e-mail.

To:	Max Johnson <m_johnson@smail.com>
From:	Shelly Preston <shelly_preston@ejpublishing.com>
Subject:	Book Feedback
Date:	28 October

Dear Mr. Johnson,

Thank you very much for sending us the draft of your new book, *Over the Moon*. I really enjoyed the storyline and the development of the characters. However, I thought that it might be easier for readers if the background story of Sharon's character was written more clearly. I also commented on some other points that may need changes. Please read the attached file to see my comments.

I would like you to review the points and change them if it is necessary. Could you send the revised version by the end of next week? Otherwise, we cannot publish your book according to the schedule.

Sincerely,

Shelly Preston
Editor in chief, EJ Publishing

28. Who most likely is Mr. Johnson?
(A) A critic
(B) An author
(C) An editor
(D) A journalist

29. The word "characters" in paragraph 1, line 2, is closest in meaning to
(A) letters
(B) roles
(C) positions
(D) copies

30. What is Mr. Johnson asked to do?
(A) Review a contract
(B) Confirm a meeting time
(C) Introduce writing rules
(D) Check an attached file

TOEIC
Vocabularies & Phrases

Unit 12 Finance

次のUnit 12に登場するTOEIC頻出語句＆フレーズです。

| Step 1 | 意味を確認した上で、音声に続いて音読してみましょう。 |
| Step 2 | 再度音声を聞きながら、意味を思い出してみましょう。 |

🎧 DL420　◉ CD4-58

□□□ account	□□□ 名口座
□□□ budget	□□□ 名予算
□□□ cash	□□□ 名現金
□□□ charge	□□□ 名料金、責任　動請求する
□□□ earn	□□□ 動稼ぐ
□□□ economy	□□□ 名経済、景気
□□□ estimate	□□□ 名見積もり　動見積もる
□□□ expense	□□□ 名経費、費用
□□□ figure	□□□ 名数字、金額
□□□ fund	□□□ 名資金　動資金を出す
□□□ fund-raising	□□□ 名資金集め　形資金集めの
□□□ invoice	□□□ 名請求書、送り状
□□□ merger	□□□ 名合併
□□□ payment	□□□ 名支払い
□□□ profit	□□□ 名利益
□□□ revenue	□□□ 名収入、収益
□□□ saving	□□□ 名貯金、預金、節約
□□□ stockholder	□□□ 名株主
□□□ tax	□□□ 名税金
□□□ withdraw	□□□ 動引き出す、撤退する

Unit 12 Finance

学習目標
- ☐ 「財務」に関する語句・表現を覚える
- ☐ 接続詞・前置詞を学ぶ

PART 1 写真描写問題

光景④ 抽象的な言い換えパターン

写真内の「物」に対しても、抽象的な表現が使われることがあります。

Some **vehicles** are stuck in traffic.（数台の車両が渋滞につかまっている）

例えば、車やオートバイが写っている写真では、carやmotorbikeという具体的な表現の他に、vehicle（乗り物、車両）という抽象的な表現も使われるので注意しましょう。

Practice! CheckLink DL 421 CD4-59

音声を聞いて空所の語句を書き取り、写真を最も適切に表す選択肢を選びましょう。

(A) There's some _____ _____ the table.
(B) A _____ is arranged on the _____.
(C) There are some _____ on the _____.
(D) A _____ is set in the _____.

PART 2 応答問題

依頼・許可

「…していただけますか」のように相手に依頼をする場合や、「…してもいいですか」のように相手に許可を得る場合には、以下のような表現が使われます。

依頼：Can you ...? / Could you ...? / Would you mind ...? / Please ....

許可：May I ...? / Can I ...? / Would you mind if I ...?

Practice! CheckLink DL422 ~ 423 CD4-60 ~ CD4-61

音声を聞いて空所の語句を書き取り、最も適切な応答の選択肢を選びましょう。

1. _____ you _____ me _____ to open a bank _____?
(A) No, that's a _____ account.
(B) You don't need an _____.
(C) _____, I can _____ you with that.

2. _____ I _____ the _____ report _____ today?
(A) No, the _____ has passed.
(B) We have a _____ _____.
(C) The _____ isn't included.

PART 3 会話問題

会話の内容の理由・原因を理解する

Part 3でよく出題される会話の内容の理由や原因としては、「話し手が電話をかけた理由」「何かを依頼している理由」「喜んだりがっかりしたりしている理由」「会議・イベントを開催または延期する理由・原因」などがあります。設問の先読みをし、なぜそのような状況に話し手たちが置かれているのか、問われる内容の前後の話を集中して聞きましょう。

Practice!

音声を聞いて空所の語句を書き取り、設問に対する最も適切な選択肢を選びましょう。

1. CheckLink DL 424 CD4-62

M: Hello, this is Kurt Sampson from Santos _____. I'm calling to _____ you know about our new _____ service. Is this a good time to _____?

W: Hi, Mr. Sampson. Can you _____ _____ the service?

Why is the man calling?

(A) To ask for a service charge

(B) To report a system problem

(C) To introduce a new service

(D) To confirm an invoice number

2. CheckLink DL 425 CD4-63

W: Hi John. I'm _____ _____ I can't start the project to _____ the old ATMs.

M: Hi Maria. _____, that isn't _____ our _____.

Why is the woman unable to begin the project?

(A) Its cost is too high.

(B) It takes time to finish.

(C) Its priority is low.

(D) It contains errors.

> **トークの内容の理由・原因を理解する**
> Part 4でよく出題されるトークの内容の理由や原因としては、「電話のメッセージを残す理由」「予定が変更される理由」「遅れが生じている原因」「ウェブサイトを見るように促されている理由」などがあります。設問の先読みから得たキーワードをもとにトーク内の関連箇所を把握し、話し手や聞き手がなぜそのような状況に置かれているのか理解しましょう。

Practice!

音声を聞いて空所の語句を書き取り、設問に対する最も適切な選択肢を選びましょう。

1.　　　　　　　　　　　　　CheckLink　　DL 426　　CD4-64

I'm calling about the _____ we sent yesterday. We _____ that it _____ _____ in the price. Could you please _____ me _____ to discuss it?

Why did the speaker call?

(A) To apologize for a delay

(B) To inform the listener of a mistake

(C) To reschedule an appointment

(D) To provide information about a product

2.　　　　　　　　　　　　　CheckLink　　DL 427　　CD4-65

The _____ party with _____ is _____ for next week. Please _____ our Web site to _____ the detailed _____ and place.

Why should listeners visit a Web site?

(A) To download a brochure

(B) To make an inquiry

(C) To fill out a form

(D) To view a schedule

PART 5 短文穴埋め問題

接続詞・前置詞
接続詞と前置詞では後ろに続くものが異なります。空所の後ろに主語と動詞が含まれる文が続いていれば接続詞を、名詞（句）だけが続いていれば前置詞を選びましょう。

Practice! CheckLink DL428 ~ 431 CD4-66

空所に入る正しい語句を選んで書き、文を完成させましょう。その後で、正解の根拠となる部分に下線を引きましょう。

1. _____ the bad economy, many companies are running out of funds.
   (A) Because   (B) Though   (C) Due to   (D) So

2. A corporate merger was proposed _____ the two companies were having a meeting.
   (A) during   (B) but   (C) unless   (D) while

3. _____ the limited advertising budget, the sales figures went up.
   (A) Despite   (B) Because of   (C) Although   (D) When

4. _____ the estimate from the company was reasonable, we decided to make a contract.
   (A) Owing to   (B) Since   (C) Even though   (D) Instead of

PART 6 長文穴埋め問題

接続表現③まとめ
TOEICで出題される主な接続表現には以下のようなものがあります。
therefore / as a result（原因・結果）、moreover / in addition / also（追加情報）、however / on the other hand（逆接）、alternatively / instead（代替手段）、otherwise（実施しない場合の結果）、for example / in particular（具体例）、first / then / finally（話の順序）

Practice! CheckLink DL432 ~ 433 CD4-67 ~ CD4-68

空所に入る正しい語句を選んで書き、文書を完成させましょう。その後で、正解の根拠となる部分に下線を引きましょう。

1. We have earned $10,000 for our research budget at the fund-raising event. _____, we still need some more funds to complete the research.

(A) However   (B) For example   (C) Otherwise   (D) Therefore

2. You can submit your expense report online. _____ , you can bring it to the accounting department in person.

(A) In particular   (B) As a result   (C) Finally   (D) Alternatively

NOT問題② 情報が並列されていない場合

What is NOT mentioned about ...?（…について述べられていないことは何ですか）のような設問の場合、不正解の3つの選択肢は本文に書かれてあり、書かれていないものが正解になります。例えば、本文にThere was a mistake in the expense report.とあり、選択肢にThe expense report was wrong.と書かれてあれば、その選択肢はNOT問題では不正解になります。なお、情報が散らばっている場合は解答に時間がかかりやすくなるので注意が必要です。

Practice!　　　　CheckLink　　DL 434　　CD4-69

文書を読んで、設問に対する最も適切な選択肢を選びましょう。その後で、正解の根拠となる部分にそれぞれ下線を引きましょう。

RB Motors Invoice		
Date: February 4		
Customer: Chris Lucas, Lucas Delivery Services		
Vehicle Information: Type: Motorbike / Make: Berttoni / Model: 380 E		
Work done:	• Chain replacement	$30
	• Front and rear brake adjustment	$25
	• Front and rear wheel tuning	$35
	Total cost with tax	$99.00
Payment method: Credit card (Payment will be withdrawn from your account at the end of March.)		
Notes: The battery is currently working properly, but for the next maintenance in six months it should be replaced. We will send you a notice in July regarding this.		

1. What is NOT done by RB Motors?

(A) Balancing wheels

(B) Changing the brake setting

(C) Installing a new chain

(D) Replacing a battery

2. What is suggested about the invoice?

(A) The fee will be paid in cash.

(B) Mr. Lucas will be contacted by RB Motors.

(C) The taxes are not included in the price.

(D) A company car has been repaired.

PART 1

 CheckLink   DL435 ~ 436   CD4-70 ~ CD4-71

Select the one statement that best describes what you see in the picture.

1.

Ⓐ Ⓑ Ⓒ Ⓓ

2.

Ⓐ Ⓑ Ⓒ Ⓓ

PART 2

 CheckLink   DL437 ~ 443   CD4-72 ~ CD4-78

Select the best response to the question or statement.

3. Mark your answer on your answer sheet.   Ⓐ Ⓑ Ⓒ

4. Mark your answer on your answer sheet.   Ⓐ Ⓑ Ⓒ

5. Mark your answer on your answer sheet.   Ⓐ Ⓑ Ⓒ

6. Mark your answer on your answer sheet.   Ⓐ Ⓑ Ⓒ

7. Mark your answer on your answer sheet.   Ⓐ Ⓑ Ⓒ

8. Mark your answer on your answer sheet.   Ⓐ Ⓑ Ⓒ

9. Mark your answer on your answer sheet.   Ⓐ Ⓑ Ⓒ

PART 3

CheckLink DL444 ~ 445 CD4-79 ~ CD4-80

Select the best response to each question.

10. Why is the man calling?
    (A) To schedule an appointment
    (B) To provide some information
    (C) To make a payment
    (D) To receive a cash bonus

11. Why does the woman thank the man?
    (A) He made a quick response.
    (B) He cleaned her house.
    (C) He arranged a meeting time.
    (D) He sent her a document.

12. What does the man offer to do?
    (A) Speak to his manager
    (B) Give a refund
    (C) Call another location
    (D) Lower the price

PART 4

CheckLink DL446 ~ 447 CD4-81 ~ CD4-82

Select the best response to each question.

13. Who most likely is the speaker calling?
    (A) A bank
    (B) A language school
    (C) An accounting firm
    (D) A publisher

14. What will the speaker do this month?
    (A) Write a monthly report
    (B) Make a presentation
    (C) Obtain some funds
    (D) Discuss sales techniques

15. Why does the speaker request a return call?
    (A) To achieve a profit goal
    (B) To talk about a merger
    (C) To correct a report
    (D) To reduce expenses

PART 5

Select the best answer to complete the sentence.

16. Mr. Davis receives support from
stockholders ------- his excellent
business results.
(A) due to
(B) in spite of
(C) but
(D) because

17. It is difficult for small businesses to
earn enough profits ------- the
economy is slowing down.
(A) although
(B) during
(C) while
(D) until

18. ------- the high rent, a lot of
companies have an office downtown.
(A) Even though
(B) Despite
(C) During
(D) When

19. Business trips will be reduced -------
the company's new policy for cost
savings.
(A) so
(B) because of
(C) instead of
(D) since

20. Companies are charged for travel
expenses ------- employees submit a
report for them.
(A) in case of
(B) although
(C) if
(D) among

21. ------- the sales figures were high,
the profit after tax was relatively low.
(A) Though
(B) Because
(C) In spite of
(D) Along

22. ------- the month of March, all the
accountants are busy preparing an
annual financial report.
(A) Even
(B) While
(C) As
(D) During

23. People can withdraw money from
ATMs only in the morning, ------- the
machines will receive maintenance.
(A) owing to
(B) in case of
(C) so
(D) since

PART 6

Select the best answer to complete the text.

Questions 24-27 refer to the following article.

Marshall Bank CEO Jeff Harrison announced today that the company and Midtown Bank have agreed upon a merger. -------, the new company is set to
24.
become the country's top banking service. The ------- of the merger have not
25.
been finalized, though all stockholders for both banks have been informed of the agreement.

Midtown Bank CEO Taylor Gibbs added that she ------- because the increased
26.
revenue will give them more business opportunities. -------. They will be
27.
announced at a later date.

---

24. (A) However
    (B) Otherwise
    (C) First
    (D) As a result

25. (A) details
    (B) fund
    (C) decision
    (D) savings

26. (A) was excited
    (B) excites
    (C) was exciting
    (D) excited

27. (A) A merger talk was held at the Western Hotel.
    (B) Stockholders attended an annual meeting.
    (C) Some branches will be combined in the future.
    (D) The economy seems to be expanding.

Select the best answer for each question.

Questions 28-32 refer to the following notice and e-mail.

The Mason Crows baseball team is looking for sponsorship as part of our fund-raising efforts. The sponsorship package comes in four levels, Bronze, Silver, Gold, and Platinum. With the exception of Bronze level sponsors, the name of sponsors will appear on the team's Web site, in the stadium or on the uniform, depending on the level.

Level	Web site	Stadium	Uniform	Cost (tax included)
Bronze	—	—	—	$100
Silver	✔	—	—	$1,000
Gold	✔	✔	—	$10,000
Platinum	✔	✔	✔	$50,000

The team will also provide complimentary tickets for sponsors and their families.

By sponsoring the team, you will help the local economy. If you are interested in sponsoring the team or have any inquiries, please contact Marv Taylor by phone, 949-555-0408, or by e-mail, mtaylor@masoncrows.com.

To:	Marv Taylor
From:	Fred Walker
Date:	March 5
Subject:	Team Sponsorship

Dear Mr. Taylor,

Hello, my name is Fred Walker from H2O Drinks. We have a question about your sponsorship. We cannot afford to pay $50,000 because of our budget. However, we want our company name to be seen in your stadium. Could you tell me where exactly the name will be shown? We also would like to know how many tickets we will get for our employees. I am looking forward to hearing from you.

Best regards,

Fred Walker

Public Relations Manager, H2O Drinks

28. What is the purpose of the notice?
   (A) To receive a payment
   (B) To gather necessary funds
   (C) To estimate an expense
   (D) To show financial figures

29. In the notice, the word
   "complimentary" in paragraph 2,
   line 1, is closest in meaning to
   (A) favorable
   (B) free
   (C) reasonable
   (D) group

30. What level will Mr. Walker likely
   choose?
   (A) Bronze
   (B) Silver
   (C) Gold
   (D) Platinum

31. What does Mr. Walker ask Mr.
   Taylor?
   (A) An area to display a company
       name
   (B) A price of a sponsorship level
   (C) When a ticket will be sent
   (D) A fund-raising party

32. What is NOT suggested about H2O
   Drinks?
   (A) It has a budget for sponsorship.
   (B) It is interested in baseball games.
   (C) It wants more public attention.
   (D) It earned more profits than last
       year.

TOEIC
Vocabularies & Phrases

Unit 13　**Meetings**

次のUnit 13に登場するTOEIC頻出語句＆フレーズです。

Step 1　意味を確認した上で、音声に続いて音読してみましょう。
Step 2　再度音声を聞きながら、意味を思い出してみましょう。

🎧 DL458　💿 CD5-02

□□□ accept	□□□	動受け入れる
□□□ agenda	□□□	名議題
□□□ appointment	□□□	名予約、約束
□□□ arrange	□□□	動手配する、配置する
□□□ attend	□□□	動出席する
□□□ conference	□□□	名（大きな）会議
□□□ contact	□□□	名連絡　動連絡する
□□□ demonstration	□□□	名実演
□□□ distribute	□□□	動配布する
□□□ material	□□□	名資料、材料
□□□ minutes	□□□	名議事録
□□□ persuade	□□□	動説得する
□□□ postpone	□□□	動延期する
□□□ productive	□□□	形生産的な
□□□ proposal	□□□	名提案
□□□ reject	□□□	動却下する
□□□ reschedule	□□□	動予定を変更する
□□□ revise	□□□	動修正する
□□□ suggestion	□□□	名提案
□□□ summary	□□□	名要約、まとめ

PART 1 写真描写問題

人物の動作⑥ 推測するパターン

写真の状況から推測できる人物の動作も正解となることがあります。

　A man is **working** at his desk.（男性がデスクで働いている）

例えば、椅子に座っている場合、オフィスなら working、バス停の前なら waiting、公園のベンチなら resting など、その状況から推測できる動作が正解になります。

Practice!

CheckLink　DL 459　CD5-03

音声を聞いて空所の語句を書き取り、写真を最も適切に表す選択肢を選びましょう。

(A) A woman is _____ _____.

(B) A woman is _____ at the

　　_____.

(C) Some people are _____

　　a _____.

(D) Some people are _____

　　some _____.

PART 2 応答問題

提案・勧誘

「…はどうですか」「…しませんか」と提案や勧誘をする場合、Why don't you ...? / How about ...? / Would you like to ...? / Would you like me to ...? などが使われます。

Practice!

CheckLink　DL460 ~ 461　CD5-04　~　CD5-05

音声を聞いて空所の語句を書き取り、最も適切な応答の選択肢を選びましょう。

1. _____ you like _____ to _____ the _____ of this meeting?

(A) Yes, that _____ be _____.

(B) A few minutes are _____.

(C) The meeting was _____.

2. _____ _____ we _____ the _____ with Mr. Perry?

(A) I haven't _____ the _____ yet.

(B) But I'm only _____ this afternoon.

(C) _____ it's too old.

PART 3 会話問題

会話の話し手の次の行動やこれから起こることに注目する

Part 3では、話し手が次に取る行動や、これから行われることなど、未来の出来事についてもよく問われます。問題や依頼事項に対して話し手が起こす行動や、今後予定されている新製品発売や重要な会議など、いつ誰が何を行うかについて注目しましょう。

Practice!

音声を聞いて空所の語句を書き取り、設問に対する最も適切な選択肢を選びましょう。

1.   CheckLink   DL 462   CD5-06

M: Hi, Ellen. Have you _____ the _____ of yesterday's _____ meeting?

W: Hi, Greg. I'm _____ done. I'll _____ you know as _____ as I finish.

What will the woman probably do next?

(A) Finish up a document

(B) Contact a client

(C) Arrange a new meeting

(D) Accept a suggestion

2.   CheckLink   DL 463   CD5-07

W: How much did you _____ _____ with the _____ for Friday's _____ meeting?

M: Well, we're making a final _____ about the _____.

What is scheduled to happen on Friday?

(A) A meeting room will be renovated.

(B) A meeting agenda will be revised.

(C) A staff meeting will be held.

(D) Some equipment will be installed.

PART 4 説明文問題

> **トークの話し手・聞き手の次の行動やこれから起こることに注目する**
> Part 4では、話し手だけでなく、聞き手が次に取る行動についても問われます。会議中に参加者へ作業の指示が出たり、留守番電話のメッセージに依頼事項が含まれたり、聞き手が取る行動についても注目しましょう。

Practice!

音声を聞いて空所の語句を書き取り、設問に対する最も適切な選択肢を選びましょう。

1.   ⟳CheckLink 🎧 DL 464 ◎CD5-08

For today's agenda, we'll _____ our _____ to _____ new projectors in _____ meeting room. But let me _____ you _____ to use the projector first.

What will the speaker do next?
(A) Introduce a new employee
(B) Distribute a manual
(C) Give a demonstration
(D) Change a room layout

2.   ⟳CheckLink 🎧 DL 465 ◎CD5-09

We're _____ changing our _____ due to a _____ in costs. I'd like your _____ on this _____. Please e-mail your _____ by next Monday.

What will listeners probably do by next Monday?
(A) Propose their ideas
(B) Change a supplier
(C) Revise a meeting summary
(D) Reduce production costs

PART 5 短文穴埋め問題

> **関係代名詞**
> 関係代名詞は、空所の前の語句が「人」か「人以外」かで次のように使い分けます。
> 空所の後ろに動詞が続く➡人：whoまたはthat　人以外：whichまたはthat
> 空所の後ろに名詞が続き、空所の前の語句と所有関係にある➡人：whose　人以外：whose
> 空所の後ろに目的語のない文が続く➡人：whomまたはwho　人以外：whichまたはthat

Practice! CheckLink DL466 ~ 469 CD5-10

空所に入る正しい語句を選んで書き、文を完成させましょう。その後で、正解の根拠となる部分に下線を引きましょう。

1. Mr. Dunlop, _____ made the proposal, is a reliable and efficient employee.
(A) who   (B) which   (C) whose   (D) whom

2. There is a monthly meeting, _____ is held at the corporate headquarters.
(A) who   (B) whose   (C) whom   (D) which

3. We arranged a meeting with Mr. Abbot, _____ business is market research.
(A) whose   (B) that   (C) who   (D) which

4. The meeting material _____ Catherine made was quite easy to understand.
(A) whom   (B) who   (C) which   (D) whose

PART 6 長文穴埋め問題

文選択問題① 話の流れを意識する
Part 6 では空所に入る適切な文を選択する問題があります。概要が述べられた後に詳細へと話が進んでいくなど、話の流れを意識して文を選択しましょう。

Practice! CheckLink DL470 ~ 471 CD5-11 ~ CD5-12

空所に入る正しい語句を選んで書き、文書を完成させましょう。その後で、正解の根拠となる部分に下線を引きましょう。

1. _____. Attached are the minutes of the meeting. Please read through them to see if there are any mistakes.

(A) Let me know if there is any problem.
(B) You may revise them if necessary.
(C) Thanks for coming to the meeting yesterday.
(D) Unfortunately, it was rejected.

2. In June, we will hold a department meeting. I would like to know how many people will come. _____.

(A) Please e-mail me if you can attend.
(B) Some people took part in the conference.
(C) There will be an opening of a department.
(D) The meeting will be rescheduled.

意図問題② 状況をイメージする

「テキストメッセージのやり取り」や「オンラインチャットの話し合い」では、書き手がなぜそのようなメッセージを送ったかについて問われます。該当するメッセージの直前のやりとりにヒントが出てくることが多いですが、メッセージ自体が遠回しな言い方をしている場合もあります。書き手たちの置かれている状況をイメージし、そのメッセージが何を言おうとしているか考えましょう。

Practice!

CheckLink　DL 472　CD5-13

文書を読んで、設問に対する最も適切な選択肢を選びましょう。その後で、正解の根拠となる部分にそれぞれ下線を引きましょう。

Frank Ashley [10:15 A.M.]	Hi, Lucy. I'm now in our client's office at FTG Manufacturing.
Lucy Kershaw [10:16 A.M.]	Hi, Frank. What happened?
Frank Ashley [10:17 A.M.]	I was supposed to attend a meeting with Mason's Factory after this, but it's taking longer than we expected.
Lucy Kershaw [10:18 A.M.]	I see. Do you think it'll end soon?
Frank Ashley [10:19 A.M.]	We haven't discussed the main point yet.
Lucy Kershaw [10:21 A.M.]	OK. Should I go instead of you?
Frank Ashley [10:23 A.M.]	That would be great. I'll send you the details of today's meeting. Can you e-mail the minutes after the meeting?
Lucy Kershaw [10:24 A.M.]	No problem.

1. At 10:19 A.M., what does Mr. Ashley most likely mean when he writes, "We haven't discussed the main point yet"?

   (A) He is holding a brief discussion.
   (B) It will take more time to finish the meeting.
   (C) A meeting started a little late.
   (D) A document included too many contents.

2. What is Ms. Kershaw asked to do?

   (A) Persuade a client
   (B) Postpone a meeting
   (C) Call a supervisor
   (D) Send a document

TOEIC
Mini Test

PART 1

 CheckLink DL473 ~ 474 CD5-14 ~ CD5-15

Select the one statement that best describes what you see in the picture.

1.

Ⓐ Ⓑ Ⓒ Ⓓ

2.

Ⓐ Ⓑ Ⓒ Ⓓ

PART 2

 CheckLink DL475 ~ 481 CD5-16 ~ CD5-22

Select the best response to the question or statement.

3. Mark your answer on your answer sheet. Ⓐ Ⓑ Ⓒ

4. Mark your answer on your answer sheet. Ⓐ Ⓑ Ⓒ

5. Mark your answer on your answer sheet. Ⓐ Ⓑ Ⓒ

6. Mark your answer on your answer sheet. Ⓐ Ⓑ Ⓒ

7. Mark your answer on your answer sheet. Ⓐ Ⓑ Ⓒ

8. Mark your answer on your answer sheet. Ⓐ Ⓑ Ⓒ

9. Mark your answer on your answer sheet. Ⓐ Ⓑ Ⓒ

PART 3

Select the best response to each question.

10. What is the conversation mainly about?
(A) Handling a customer complaint
(B) Preparing for a meeting
(C) Revising a document
(D) Changing a meeting agenda

11. What is the problem?
(A) Some data is not available.
(B) A meeting has been canceled.
(C) A deadline has passed.
(D) A proposal was rejected.

12. What does the man say he will do later?
(A) Distribute some material
(B) Persuade a client
(C) Postpone a presentation
(D) Get in touch with a coworker

PART 4

Select the best response to each question.

13. Who most likely are the listeners?
(A) Factory workers
(B) Sales representatives
(C) Event planners
(D) Security officers

14. What are the listeners asked to do?
(A) Begin a discussion
(B) Submit their ideas
(C) Write down a summary
(D) Meet a client

15. What will the listeners hear about next?
(A) Monthly sales results
(B) A product demonstration
(C) A guest speaker's speech
(D) International business opportunities

Select the best answer to complete the sentence.

16. LLT Industries has changed the offer
------- was rejected by its client.
(A) who
(B) which
(C) whose
(D) whom

17. The appointment with Mr. Walsh,
------- company provides financial
services, was postponed.
(A) whose
(B) who
(C) that
(D) which

18. The meeting minutes ------- a new
employee made were approved by a
supervisor.
(A) whom
(B) who
(C) that
(D) whose

19. Ms. Hallows, ------- is responsible
for marketing, was persuaded to
accept the suggestion.
(A) whom
(B) whose
(C) which
(D) who

20. All the executives attended the
meeting ------- agenda included
personnel change.
(A) whose
(B) that
(C) whom
(D) which

21. Dyson Legal Office and its client had
a brief meeting, ------- was highly
productive.
(A) who
(B) whose
(C) which
(D) whom

22. We made a final decision during the
discussion with Ms. Nelson, -------
we hired as a business consultant.
(A) whom
(B) which
(C) whose
(D) what

23. Those ------- could not take part in
the conference can watch a recorded
video later.
(A) which
(B) whom
(C) who
(D) whose

Select the best answer to complete the text.

Questions 24-27 refer to the following e-mail.

To: Tony Swann <tonyswann@alltools.com>
From: Sarah North <sarahnorth@northtec.com>
Date: April 23
Subject: Reschedule the meeting

Dear Mr. Swann,

Thank you for the meeting yesterday. We scheduled the next meeting on Monday at 3 P.M. -------, I have some urgent business to take care of. I would like to
24.
reschedule the meeting sometime next week. Could you tell me your -------
25.
dates and times? After Monday we are open to meeting at any time. At that time we would like to go over the possibility of ------- your latest projectors and
26.
presentation tools. -------.
27.

Regards,
Sarah North

---

24. (A) Therefore
(B) Moreover
(C) Unfortunately
(D) Alternatively

25. (A) limited
(B) productive
(C) previous
(D) available

26. (A) purchasing
(B) purchase
(C) purchased
(D) to purchase

27. (A) The next appointment will be postponed.
(B) I look forward to hearing from you.
(C) Here is the summary of the meeting.
(D) We hope you accept our material.

PART 7

Select the best answer for each question.

Questions 28-30 refer to the following online chat discussion.

1:00 P.M. Natalia Brown

Hi everyone. Have you finished installing the new video conferencing software? You'll need it for the branch managers meeting at 3 P.M.

1:01 P.M. Marsha Downing

I had a meeting all morning. I'll check it out right now.

1:02 P.M. Jeff Andrews

I've already installed it. I'm ready for the meeting.

1:03 P.M. Eric Murdoch

I tried to download the file to install it, but couldn't.

1:04 P.M. Natalia Brown

OK. Just a moment. I'll check with the IT department ...

1:07 P.M. Natalia Brown

Eric, please try it again. Now you have permission to access the file.

1:08 P.M. Eric Murdoch

Oh, thanks. I'll do it again.

1:09 P.M. Marsha Downing

I just finished installing it.

---

28. At 1:01 P.M., what does Ms. Downing most likely mean when she writes, "I had a meeting all morning"?
(A) She had a meeting with branch managers.
(B) She finished arranging an appointment.
(C) She conducted a product demonstration.
(D) She has not installed the software.

29. Why does Ms. Brown contact the IT department?
(A) To borrow a new computer
(B) To ask about a technical issue
(C) To open a company e-mail account
(D) To request a monthly inspection

30. What will Mr. Murdoch most likely do next?
(A) Visit the IT department
(B) Take part in a meeting
(C) Download a file
(D) Distribute a manual

TOEIC
Vocabularies & Phrases

Unit 14　**Sales & Marketing**

次のUnit 14に登場するTOEIC頻出語句＆フレーズです。

Step 1　意味を確認した上で、音声に続いて音読してみましょう。

Step 2　再度音声を聞きながら、意味を思い出してみましょう。

DL496　CD5-30

□□□ analyze	□□□ 動分析する
□□□ competition	□□□ 名競争
□□□ competitive	□□□ 形競争力のある、競争の激しい
□□□ conduct	□□□ 動行う、実施する
□□□ decline	□□□ 名減少　動減少する
□□□ decrease	□□□ 名減少　動低下する、低下させる
□□□ demand	□□□ 名需要、要求　動要求する
□□□ expand	□□□ 動拡大する
□□□ export	□□□ 名輸出　動輸出する
□□□ import	□□□ 名輸入　動輸入する
□□□ increase	□□□ 名増加　動増える、増やす
□□□ industry	□□□ 名産業、業界
□□□ launch	□□□ 名開始、発売　動始める、発売する
□□□ promotional	□□□ 形販売促進の
□□□ questionnaire	□□□ 名アンケート（用紙）
□□□ reduce	□□□ 動減らす、縮小する
□□□ research	□□□ 名研究、調査　動研究する、調査する
□□□ result	□□□ 名結果
□□□ strategy	□□□ 名戦略、計画
□□□ survey	□□□ 名調査　動調査する

Unit 14 Sales & Marketing

PART 1 写真描写問題

光景⑤ 現在完了形の受動態パターン

「物」が主語の場合、現在完了形の受動態が使われることもあります。

Some watches **have been arranged** for display.（腕時計が展示用に並べられている）

「物」が主語の場合、are arrangedのように現在形の受動態で状態を表すことが多いですが、上記のように現在完了形の受動態を使って完了した動作を表すこともできます。

Practice!

CheckLink　DL 497　CD5-31

音声を聞いて空所の語句を書き取り、写真を最も適切に表す選択肢を選びましょう。

(A) Shoes have been _____ next to a _____.

(B) _____ has been _____ on shelves.

(C) Some bags have been _____ from the _____.

(D) Items have been _____ in a shopping _____.

PART 2 応答問題

選択疑問文

「AですかそれともBですか」のような選択疑問文の応答は、「Aです」「Bです」「両方です」「どちらでもいいです」のほか、「Cです」など予想外の場合もあります。

Practice!

CheckLink　DL498～499　CD5-32　～　CD5-33

音声を聞いて空所の語句を書き取り、最も適切な応答の選択肢を選びましょう。

1. _____ we _____ the _____ _____ this month or next month?

(A) That's very _____.

(B) The sales _____ will be better.

(C) _____ do it _____ month.

2. Can you _____ _____ the _____ today, or will you _____ more time?

(A) I've just _____ the results to you.

(B) The _____ was _____ last week.

(C) The _____ and development data.

PART 3 会話問題

Practice!

音声を聞いて空所の語句を書き取り、設問に対する最も適切な選択肢を選びましょう。

1.   CheckLink   DL 500   CD5-34

M: Sales _____ _____. Everyone wants to _____ _____ that _____.

W: Some people _____ me about it, so I'll give a presentation tomorrow.

What does the woman imply when she says, "I'll give a presentation tomorrow"?

(A) She has an appointment with a customer.

(B) She knows the reason for the increase in sales.

(C) She has completed a questionnaire.

(D) She will develop a marketing tool.

2.   CheckLink   DL 501   CD5-35

M: As you _____, we're having a meeting to analyze some markets. Their sales _____ were really _____.

W: OK, I'll _____ the discussion _____, but _____ me call a client first.

What does the man imply when he says, "we're having a meeting to analyze some markets"?

(A) He was asked to conduct some research.

(B) He has to reduce some marketing budgets.

(C) He wants the woman to join a group.

(D) He will have to report to a client.

トークの展開から間接的な発言の意図を理解する

Part 4においても、What does the speaker imply when he says, "it's Mr. Green's research"? (話し手は"it's Mr. Green's research"という発言で、何を示唆しています か) のように、発言の意図が問われます。間接的な発言の前後の文脈から、直接的な 意味を理解しましょう。

Practice!

音声を聞いて空所の語句を書き取り、設問に対する最も適切な選択肢を選びましょう。

1.   ↻CheckLink 🎧 DL 502 ◎ CD5-36

Do you think the sales strategy is working? _____, we _____ the _____ _____ in March. We _____ do something _____.

What does the speaker imply when he says, "Do you think the sales strategy is working"?

(A) He thinks a strategy needs a change.

(B) He knew there was a mistake.

(C) He will meet some customers.

(D) He wants to continue his research.

2.   ↻CheckLink 🎧 DL 503 ◎ CD5-37

_____ you know, our _____ is _____ _____. TLD Tech and two other companies will _____ a new _____ next month. We can't change this situation.

What does the speaker imply when she says, "We can't change this situation"?

(A) She wants to export a product overseas.

(B) A financial situation has been changed.

(C) Her company needs to develop a better product.

(D) A new supervisor will be hired next month.

PART 5 短文穴埋め問題

語彙① 同じ品詞の異なる単語が並んでいる場合

Part 5 では文法の知識だけでなく、動詞、形容詞、副詞、名詞に関する語彙力も求め られます。選択肢に、(A) decline (B) analyze (C) import (D) reduceのように、同一 品詞 (ここでは動詞) で異なる単語が並んでいれば語彙力が問われる問題です。

空所に入る正しい語句を選んで書き、文を完成させましょう。その後で、正解の根拠となる部分に下線を引きましょう。

1. The annual _____ shows that customers prefer quality over price.

    (A) industry   (B) demand   (C) survey   (D) generation

2. Kevin's Appliance Store runs a _____ campaign every month.

    (A) previous   (B) promotional   (C) fluent   (D) past

3. Restaurant sales in the downtown area have declined _____ due to bad weather.

    (A) rapidly   (B) quarterly   (C) closely   (D) newly

4. FBC Services is a consulting company that _____ on marketing strategy.

    (A) imports   (B) puts   (C) advertises   (D) focuses

PART 6 長文穴埋め問題

文選択問題② 名詞・代名詞に注目する

文選択問題で選択する文に代名詞がある場合、前の文から元となる名詞を探します。空所の後ろに代名詞がある場合は、選択する文から元となる名詞を探します。

空所に入る正しい語句を選んで書き、文書を完成させましょう。その後で、正解の根拠となる部分に下線を引きましょう。

> **1.** We are going to contract with Mr. Trevor to get professional advice about market research. _____.

(A) They are expanding business overseas.

(B) It was a highly competitive market.

(C) He is an experienced consultant in this area.

(D) The new product is competitively priced.

> **2.** _____.
> Both of them have been trying to make decisions based on customer feedback.

(A) We conducted a customer satisfaction survey.

(B) A new product will be launched next month.

(C) The demand for our products is increasing.

(D) Two of our branches achieved their sales goals.

文挿入問題② 挿入する文から前後の文の内容を予測する

文挿入問題では、挿入する文の内容から前後に何が書いてあるか予測できる場合があります。挿入する文にalsoやtoo、the same thingがあれば、同様の話が前の文に書いてあると予想できます。例えば、挿入する文が**The quality of the product was also good.**であれば、その前に料金やデザインなど商品に関するよい点が書いてあると予想できます。

Practice!   CheckLink   DL 510   CD5-41

文書を読んで、設問に対する最も適切な選択肢を選びましょう。その後で、正解の根拠となる部分にそれぞれ下線を引きましょう。

Sunnyside Spa

Dear customers,

Please fill out the questionnaire below to help us make any improvements. — [1] —.

Name: Daniela Cruz   **Age:** 38   **Spa Location:** Palm Beach   **Date of visit:** July 20

5: Very good   4: Good   3: OK   2: Bad   1: Very bad

Service	5	4	③	2	1
Staff	5	4	3	②	1
Location	⑤	4	3	2	1
Price	5	④	3	2	1

Would you consider visiting our facilities in the future?   ✔ Yes   ☐ No

---

Comments: — [2] —. Overall, I enjoyed my experience at the spa. It is located in a great place along the beach with some spectacular views. — [3] —. However, when I tried to request towels, there was no staff to assist us. — [4] —. As a result, I couldn't get them. Hopefully, your staff will learn to be more helpful, and be more readily available to customers.

---

1. What is the purpose of the form?

(A) To confirm a reservation

(B) To submit a personal introduction

(C) To get feedback about services

(D) To apply for an exercise class

2. In which of the positions marked [1], [2], [3], and [4] does the following sentence best belong?

"We also thought the price was reasonable."

(A) [1]   (B) [2]   (C) [3]   (D) [4]

TOEIC
Mini Test

PART 1

CheckLink DL511 ~ 512 CD5-42 ~ CD5-43

Select the one statement that best describes what you see in the picture.

1.

Ⓐ Ⓑ Ⓒ Ⓓ

2.

Ⓐ Ⓑ Ⓒ Ⓓ

PART 2

CheckLink DL513 ~ 519 CD5-44 ~ CD5-50

Select the best response to the question or statement.

3. Mark your answer on your answer sheet. Ⓐ Ⓑ Ⓒ

4. Mark your answer on your answer sheet. Ⓐ Ⓑ Ⓒ

5. Mark your answer on your answer sheet. Ⓐ Ⓑ Ⓒ

6. Mark your answer on your answer sheet. Ⓐ Ⓑ Ⓒ

7. Mark your answer on your answer sheet. Ⓐ Ⓑ Ⓒ

8. Mark your answer on your answer sheet. Ⓐ Ⓑ Ⓒ

9. Mark your answer on your answer sheet. Ⓐ Ⓑ Ⓒ

PART 3

Select the best response to each question.

10. What are the speakers mainly discussing?
(A) Sales performance
(B) Importing parts
(C) Market competition
(D) Developing a new product

11. What does the man imply when he says, "we ran out of parts in April"?
(A) Prices of parts increased.
(B) He ordered a wrong item.
(C) A company could not make enough products.
(D) A demand for a product declined.

12. What is scheduled to happen next month?
(A) An industry conference
(B) A product launch
(C) A fund-raising dinner
(D) A promotional campaign

PART 4

Select the best response to each question.

13. What is the purpose of the talk?
(A) To select a product name
(B) To introduce a strategy
(C) To present survey results
(D) To ask for opinions

14. What does the speaker imply when she says, "You know people like such videos"?
(A) She likes to watch videos.
(B) She is concerned about competition.
(C) Videos are effective in advertisements.
(D) The listeners should act quickly.

15. What will the listeners probably do next?
(A) Answer a questionnaire
(B) Read a schedule
(C) Check a package design
(D) Visit a Web site

Select the best answer to complete the sentence.

16. Arthur Housing offers high-quality furniture at ------- prices every day.
    (A) related
    (B) interested
    (C) competitive
    (D) electronic

17. The survey shows not only food but also the service staff is highly ------- at the restaurant.
    (A) evaluated
    (B) expanded
    (C) conducted
    (D) decreased

18. It is extremely important for salespeople to handle customer ------- properly.
    (A) industries
    (B) suppliers
    (C) causes
    (D) inquiries

19. According to the report, car sales have been increasing ------- during the summer season.
    (A) deeply
    (B) newly
    (C) gradually
    (D) loudly

20. Results of questionnaires are mainly used for ------- customer needs.
    (A) reducing
    (B) promoting
    (C) transferring
    (D) analyzing

21. The sales team members are relieved because they have ------- achieved their sales goal.
    (A) already
    (B) rarely
    (C) yet
    (D) usually

22. Customers can fill out a customer satisfaction survey either in written or ------- forms.
    (A) exported
    (B) online
    (C) effective
    (D) reasonable

23. There was a ------- in ticket sales in August as a result of the temporary closure of a movie theater.
    (A) performance
    (B) decline
    (C) qualification
    (D) promotion

PART 6

Select the best answer to complete the text.

Questions 24-27 refer to the following e-mail.

To: j_strong@gscomputers.com
From: s_naysmith@gscomputers.com
Date: May 10
Subject: Sales Report

Hi Josh,

As you requested, I have attached the current sales report. Due to the ------- **24.** closing of our Sydney factory, many shipments of our printers have been delayed. Because of this, our downtown shops could not get enough printers on time. -------, total sales have fallen short of the target. -------. We should analyze **25.** **26.** why we had to close the factory ------- further delays. **27.**

Susan

---

24. (A) available
　　(B) promotional
　　(C) complimentary
　　(D) temporary

25. (A) As a result
　　(B) However
　　(C) Otherwise
　　(D) Alternatively

26. (A) The sales report was not
　　　submitted.
　　(B) They are about 4% lower than
　　　last month.
　　(C) You will send out a questionnaire.
　　(D) It was competition between
　　　industries.

27. (A) prevent
　　(B) preventing
　　(C) to prevent
　　(D) prevented

Select the best answer for each question.

Questions 28-30 refer to the following e-mail.

To:	fjoyner@radtech.com
From:	rtravis@tl_software.com
Date:	July 12
Subject:	New Marketing Application

Dear Ms. Joyner,

This is Roy Travis from TL Software. I am e-mailing you about our new version of the marketing tool you use. — [1] —. As marketing director, you will find this version more helpful to increase the sales of your tablets and computers. — [2] —. One of its newest features is to research and analyze market trends. You can create competitive sales campaigns for products that are popular and in demand. — [3] —.

We are currently visiting users to give demonstrations of the new features. — [4] —. Is there any available time for you to see us at your office? We look forward to your response.

Best regards,

Roy Travis
Senior Sales Representative, Sales Division
TL Software, Inc.

28. For what type of business does Ms. Joyner likely work?

(A) An electronic manufacturer
(B) A software company
(C) A marketing company
(D) A Web design firm

29. What does Mr. Travis offer to do?

(A) Send a software manual
(B) Show new functions
(C) Achieve sales targets
(D) Reduce a product price

30. In which of the positions marked [1], [2], [3], and [4] does the following sentence best belong?

"You can see the sales results in real time, too."

(A) [1]
(B) [2]
(C) [3]
(D) [4]

TOEIC
Vocabularies & Phrases

Unit 15 **Seminar & Workshop**

次の Unit 15 に登場する TOEIC 頻出語句＆フレーズです。

Step 1	意味を確認した上で、音声に続いて音読してみましょう。
Step 2	再度音声を聞きながら、意味を思い出してみましょう。

🎧 DL534 ◎ CD5-58

☐☐☐ accommodate	☐☐☐ 動収容する
☐☐☐ annual	☐☐☐ 形毎年恒例の
☐☐☐ auditorium	☐☐☐ 名講堂
☐☐☐ award	☐☐☐ 名賞　動授与する
☐☐☐ banquet	☐☐☐ 名宴会、晩餐会
☐☐☐ enroll	☐☐☐ 動登録する
☐☐☐ handout	☐☐☐ 名配布資料
☐☐☐ hold	☐☐☐ 動開催する、催す
☐☐☐ introduce	☐☐☐ 動紹介する
☐☐☐ lead	☐☐☐ 動率いる、主導する、指導する
☐☐☐ participate	☐☐☐ 動参加する
☐☐☐ reception	☐☐☐ 名受付、歓迎会
☐☐☐ register	☐☐☐ 動登録する
☐☐☐ seminar	☐☐☐ 名セミナー
☐☐☐ session	☐☐☐ 名集まり、会合
☐☐☐ sign up	☐☐☐ 申し込む、登録する
☐☐☐ take part in	☐☐☐ 参加する
☐☐☐ take place	☐☐☐ 行われる
☐☐☐ upcoming	☐☐☐ 形今度の、来るべき
☐☐☐ workshop	☐☐☐ 名講習会、研修

Unit 15 Seminar & Workshop

学習目標
- □ 「セミナー・研修」に関する語句・表現を覚える
- □ 語彙を学ぶ②

PART 1 写真描写問題

光景⑥ 受動態の進行形パターン

「物」が主語の場合、受動態の進行形が使われることもあります。

A seminar room **is being cleaned.**（セミナールームが掃除されているところである）

この場合、セミナールームが掃除中であれば正解ですが、ただきれいな状態であれば不正解になります。beingを聞き逃すと正解のように聞こえるので注意しましょう。

Practice!

⟲CheckLink 🎧 DL 535 ⦿ CD5-59

音声を聞いて空所の語句を書き取り、写真を最も適切に表す選択肢を選びましょう。

(A) A _____ is being _____.

(B) Some _____ are being _____.

(C) A _____ is being _____.

(D) _____ are being _____.

PART 2 応答問題

平叙文

Part 2では、文がピリオド（.）で終わる平叙文も主題されます。応答は平叙文に対する意見や情報の提示、内容に関する質問などがあります。例えば、I attended a seminar yesterday.に対し、What did you learn?のように疑問文で応答する場合もあります。

Practice!

⟲CheckLink 🎧 DL536 ~ 537 ⦿ CD5-60 ~ ⦿ CD5-61

音声を聞いて空所の語句を書き取り、最も適切な応答の選択肢を選びましょう。

1. I _____ Ms. White will _____ the _____ _____.

(A) I haven't _____ the report.

(B) She's very _____ in _____.

(C) There's a _____ desk.

2. We _____ to decide _____ we'll _____ the _____.

(A) _____ about the _____ hall?

(B) _____ next month.

(C) We'll announce the _____ winners

PART 3 会話問題

図表問題② 場所や位置関係を表す表現に注意する

図表を伴う問題では、表だけでなく地図や部屋のレイアウトなどが出題される場合があります。behind the building（建物の後ろに）、next to the entrance（入口の隣に）など、場所や位置関係を表す表現がヒントになり、正解を導き出せる場合もあります。

Practice!

音声を聞いて空所の語句を書き取り、設問に対する最も適切な選択肢を選びましょう。

1.   CheckLink DL 538 CD5-62

M: Thanks for today's _____. Where should

   I _____ the participant _____?

W: After you _____ it out, can you

   _____ the document in the box on

   the _____ table?

Look at the graphic. Where should the man submit a document?

(A) At location A

(B) At location B

(C) At location C

(D) At location D

Ⓐ Front Desk	Ⓑ Entrance
☐	Ⓒ
☐	☐
☐	Ⓓ

Tables

2.   CheckLink DL 539 CD5-63

M: I can't wait to _____ in

   the _____ training

   _____. Oh, by the way

   ... has the room been decided?

W: Yes, it's the _____

   room from the _____

   on the _____ floor.

Room 304	Room 303	Room 302	Room 301	
				Stairs

Look at the graphic. Where will the training be held?

(A) Room 301

(B) Room 302

(C) Room 303

(D) Room 304

PART 4 説明文問題

図表問題② 特徴を表す表現に注意する

トークでも地図や部屋のレイアウトなどが出題されます。the smallest room（いちばん小さな部屋）、three rows of tables（3列のテーブル）など、それぞれの選択肢の特徴を表す表現を聞き、他の選択肢との違いを理解しましょう。

Practice!

音声を聞いて空所の語句を書き取り、設問に対する最も適切な選択肢を選びましょう。

1.

🔄CheckLink 🎧 DL 540 ⊚ CD5-64

I'd like to _____ some changes to the _____. _____ a lot of people have _____ up, it'll _____ place in the _____ room on the _____ floor.

Room 801	Stairs
Room 802	
Room 803	
	Room 804

Look at the graphic. Which room will be used?

(A) Room 801
(B) Room 802
(C) Room 803
(D) Room 804

2.

🔄CheckLink 🎧 DL 541 ⊚ CD5-65

Due to the _____ of the parking lot in _____ of the building, people who _____ _____ the seminar should use the _____ parking area and the _____ entrance.

Look at the graphic. Where should seminar participants park their cars?

(A) In Parking Area 1
(B) In Parking Area 2
(C) In Parking Area 3
(D) In Parking Area 4

Parking Area 1		
Parking Area 4	(Rear Entrance) Building (Front Entrance)	Parking Area 2
	Parking Area 3	

PART 5 短文穴埋め問題

語彙② 一緒によく使われる単語の知識が求められる場合

語彙問題では、一緒によく使われる単語の知識が求められます。例えば、take part in the seminar（セミナーに参加する）という表現を知っていれば、takeが空所の場合、part inがヒントになり正解を導き出すことができます。

Practice!

空所に入る正しい語句を選んで書き、文を完成させましょう。その後で、正解の根拠となる部分に下線を引きましょう。

1. _____ were distributed to attendees at the beginning of the workshop.

   (A) Instructors   (B) Handouts   (C) Auditoriums   (D) Receptions

2. Mr. Curtis is a highly _____ instructor for the writing course.

   (A) frequent   (B) entire   (C) latest   (D) experienced

3. If you want to attend the seminar, please _____ up for it by tomorrow.

   (A) take   (B) sign   (C) introduce   (D) register

4. Leadership training can help new managers work _____ with their team members.

   (A) definitely   (B) sharply   (C) effectively   (D) recently

PART 6 長文穴埋め問題

文選択問題③ まとめ

文選択問題では、空所の前後の文と挿入文に言い換え表現があるかどうかに注目しましょう。例えば、空所の前に We need a projector. とある場合、挿入文には、projector の代わりに the device（機器）のような言い換え表現が使われる場合があります。

Practice!

空所に入る正しい語句を選んで書き、文書を完成させましょう。その後で、正解の根拠となる部分に下線を引きましょう。

1. Emily and I are preparing some handouts for the meeting management course.

   --.

(A) The annual event will be canceled.

(B) They are taking part in the course.

(C) The documents will have ten pages.

(D) We have not received the results.

2. --. In the first half, you will learn five steps for handling customer complaints properly.

(A) Terry is going to lead the seminar twice.

(B) We have a limited number of seats.

(C) The workshop is divided into two parts.

(D) She has already enrolled in the class.

複数の文書に関する問題② 文書を紐づける情報を見つける
複数の文書に関する問題には、1つの文書を読んだだけでは解答できない設問が必ず含まれます。設問内のキーワードを元に1つの文書から関連する情報を探し出し、さらにそこから新たなキーワードを見つけ、別の文書と紐づけると正解が見つかることが多いです。

Practice!

↻CheckLink　🎧 DL 548　◉ CD5-69

文書を読んで、設問に対する最も適切な選択肢を選びましょう。その後で、正解の根拠となる部分にそれぞれ下線を引きましょう。

Career Development Conference in Dallas			
June 29	Presentation Basics	**July 1**	Presentation Practice
June 30	Strategy Planning	**July 2**	Strategy Evaluation

To:　　　Michelle Wang <m_wang@digitalsolutions.com>
From:　 Thomas Smith <t_smith@digitalsolutions.com>
Subject: RE: Career Development Conference

Dear Ms. Wang,

This is Thomas Smith. I am head of sales here in the Daytona branch in Florida. Thank you for your notice about the career development conference. It sounds like a great opportunity for me to learn something new from the speakers. I'm interested in taking the course on the last day of the conference. Please use my name and e-mail address to reserve a space at this conference.

Best regards,

Thomas Smith

1. What is the purpose of the e-mail?
   (A) To request a schedule change
   (B) To sign up for a business course
   (C) To introduce an instructor
   (D) To confirm a conference date

2. Which course will Mr. Smith probably take at the conference?
   (A) Presentation Basics
   (B) Strategy Planning
   (C) Presentation Practice
   (D) Strategy Evaluation

TOEIC
Mini Test

Select the one statement that best describes what you see in the picture.

1.

Ⓐ Ⓑ Ⓒ Ⓓ

2.

Ⓐ Ⓑ Ⓒ Ⓓ

Select the best response to the question or statement.

3. Mark your answer on your answer sheet.   Ⓐ Ⓑ Ⓒ

4. Mark your answer on your answer sheet.   Ⓐ Ⓑ Ⓒ

5. Mark your answer on your answer sheet.   Ⓐ Ⓑ Ⓒ

6. Mark your answer on your answer sheet.   Ⓐ Ⓑ Ⓒ

7. Mark your answer on your answer sheet.   Ⓐ Ⓑ Ⓒ

8. Mark your answer on your answer sheet.   Ⓐ Ⓑ Ⓒ

9. Mark your answer on your answer sheet.   Ⓐ Ⓑ Ⓒ

PART 3

Select the best response to each question.

Parking Area 1	Grass Field	Parking Area 2
Auditorium	Fountain	Library
Museum	Parking Area 4	Parking Area 3

10. Who most likely is Mr. Rush?
   (A) A writer
   (B) An attendee
   (C) An instructor
   (D) A journalist

11. What does the woman suggest?
   (A) Taking the man to an event
   (B) Introducing her client
   (C) Registering for a course
   (D) Calling a reception desk

12. Look at the graphic. Where should the woman park her car?
   (A) In Parking Area 1
   (B) In Parking Area 2
   (C) In Parking Area 3
   (D) In Parking Area 4

PART 4

Select the best response to each question.

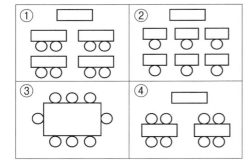

13. For whom will the training be held?
   (A) University students
   (B) Management staff
   (C) Hotel clerks
   (D) Job applicants

14. Look at the graphic. Which room arrangement should be used for the training?
   (A) Arrangement 1
   (B) Arrangement 2
   (C) Arrangement 3
   (D) Arrangement 4

15. What will the man do later?
   (A) Confirm the number of participants
   (B) Prepare handouts
   (C) Sign up for an event
   (D) Reserve a banquet room

PART 5

Select the best answer to complete the sentence.

16. Before we start the course, please
------- yourself to the other
participants.
(A) increase
(B) feature
(C) charge
(D) introduce

17. After the seminar, all the attendees
are advised to give honest -------
about the contents.
(A) awards
(B) feedback
(C) handouts
(D) selection

18. The ------- industry workshop is
scheduled to take place at the
Swingler Hotel.
(A) numerous
(B) high
(C) annual
(D) exact

19. The opening ceremony of the
international conference will be held
at a ------- renovated auditorium.
(A) mainly
(B) hopefully
(C) newly
(D) closely

20. Detailed information about the
seminar is now ------- on the Web
site.
(A) productive
(B) available
(C) excited
(D) complimentary

21. Each meeting room in the national
conference center can ------- at least
twenty people.
(A) accommodate
(B) expand
(C) participate
(D) launch

22. Most of the ------- from employees
who took part in the training session
were positive.
(A) comments
(B) facilities
(C) luggage
(D) workplaces

23. Mr. Marland and his colleagues
------- attend technical workshops to
learn the latest technology.
(A) strongly
(B) accordingly
(C) extremely
(D) regularly

Select the best answer to complete the text.

Questions 24-27 refer to the following e-mail.

From: RonaldStraw@DIP.com

To: Joseph_Lee@RAMtech.com

Date: June 2

Subject: Annual Digital Camera Conference

Dear Mr. Lee,

I would like to ------- you of our upcoming annual digital camera conference on
24.
Saturday, July 9. Last year you led a workshop regarding your company's state-
of-the-art lenses. -------. Therefore, we would like to invite you and -------
25.   **26.**
company back to participate in this event. It is set to take place in the Downtown
Expo Hall from 9 A.M. to 6 P.M. Please let us know if you are interested in -------.
27.

Best regards,
Ronald Straw
Director, Digital Images Press

---

24. (A) present
    (B) inform
    (C) solve
    (D) prepare

26. (A) our
    (B) his
    (C) your
    (D) her

25. (A) I bought an expensive camera
       recently.
    (B) Everyone enjoyed learning the
       new features.
    (C) The hall is conveniently located.
    (D) You need to register in advance.

27. (A) joins
    (B) to join
    (C) join
    (D) joining

PART 7

Select the best answer for each question.

Questions 28-32 refer to the following e-mails and schedule.

From:	MarkBerry@smartdesigns.com
To:	RitaPrice@smartdesigns.com
Date:	September 15
Subject:	Hotel Reservation for Seminar

Dear Rita,

Have you reserved rooms at the Samwell Hotel? The designers' seminar will be held at the hotel next month, so it would be convenient to stay there. If there are no rooms available, we need to make reservations at a different hotel soon. Please let me know your progress.

Sincerely,

Mark

From:	RitaPrice@smartdesigns.com
To:	MarkBerry@smartdesigns.com
Date:	September 16
Subject:	RE: Hotel Reservation for Seminar

Dear Mark,

I am so sorry I have not gotten back to you. Unfortunately, all rooms at the Samwell Hotel and other hotels around the area are full. Therefore, I have reserved rooms at the Heston Hotel, which is a little far from the Samwell Hotel. We can go to the seminar by bus. One more thing I should mention is we cannot get there before 10 a.m. due to the bus schedule, so we may miss some of the program.

Sincerely,

Rita

Time (A.M.)	Presentation (Presenter)	Time (P.M.)	Presentation (Presenter)
9:00-10:00	Web Design (Ted Benson)	1:00-2:30	Design Process (Tom York)
10:30-12:00	Logo Design (Tina Wise)	3:00-4:30	Design Trends (Lily Lipson)

Unit 15 **Seminar & Workshop** 181

28. According to the first e-mail, why does Mark contact Rita?
    (A) He wants to cancel a reservation.
    (B) He needs to have revised handouts.
    (C) He wants to know the situation.
    (D) He needs to enroll in a seminar.

29. In the first e-mail, the word "convenient" in paragraph 1, line 2, is closest in meaning to
    (A) frequent
    (B) complete
    (C) helpful
    (D) productive

30. What is suggested about the Samwell Hotel?
    (A) It is located near the Heston Hotel.
    (B) It has a large banquet hall.
    (C) It has several branches.
    (D) It will hold a seminar in October.

31. Which presentation are Mark and Rita unable to attend?
    (A) Web Design
    (B) Logo Design
    (C) Design Process
    (D) Design Trends

32. Who will lead the Logo Design session?
    (A) Ted Benson
    (B) Tina Wise
    (C) Tom York
    (D) Lily Lipson

このシールをはがすと
CheckLink 利用のための
「**教科書固有番号**」が
記載されています。

一度はがすと元に戻すことは
できませんのでご注意下さい。

▲ここからはがして下さい

4183 GIGA BOOSTER
(TOEIC)

CheckLink®

本書にはCD（別売）があります

GIGA BOOSTER FOR THE TOEIC® L&R TEST

全パート・全頻出！　TOEIC® L&R テスト実戦問題GIGA

2023年 1 月20日　初版第 1 刷発行
2023年 2 月20日　初版第 2 刷発行

著　者　　早 川 幸 治
　　　　　番 場 直 之

発行者　　福 岡 正 人

発行所　　株式会社　金 星 堂

（〒101-0051）　東京都千代田区神田神保町 3-21
　　　　Tel　（03）3263-3828（営業部）
　　　　　　　（03）3263-3997（編集部）
　　　　Fax　（03）3263-0716
　　　　https://www.kinsei-do.co.jp

編集担当　今門貴浩　　　　　　　　　　　　　Printed in Japan
印刷所・製本所／大日本印刷株式会社

ISBN978-4-7647-4183-6　C1082